Lawrence E. Shapiro

GAMES
TO GROW ON

activities to help children
learn self-control

A SPECTRUM BOOK

Prentice-Hall, Inc.
Englewood Cliffs, New Jersey 07632

Library of Congress Cataloging in Publication Data

Shapiro, Lawrence E
    Games to grow on.

    (A Spectrum Book)
    Bibliography: p.
    Includes index.
        1. Educational games.   2. Self-control—Study
and Teaching.   3. Classroom management.   4. Problem
children—Education.   I. Title.
LB1029.G3S5   372.13   ´   80-26773
ISBN 0—13—346148—3
ISBN 0—13—346130—0 (pbk.)

*To the memory of my wife, Ellen,
and to our daughter, Jessica.*

© 1981 by Prentice-Hall, Inc., Englewood Cliffs, New Jersey 07632

A SPECTRUM BOOK

Editorial/production supervision and interior design by Cyndy Lyle
Manufacturing buyer Cathie Lenard
Art production by Mary Greey
Cover design by Judith Kazdym Leeds

10 9 8 7 6 5 4 3 2 1

Printed in the United States of America

Prentice-Hall International, Inc., *London*
Prentice-Hall of Australia Pty. Limited, *Sydney*
Prentice-Hall of Canada, Ltd., *Toronto*
Prentice-Hall of India Private Limited, *New Delhi*
Prentice-Hall of Japan, Inc., *Tokyo*
Prentice-Hall of Southeast Asia Pte. Ltd., *Singapore*
Whitehall Books Limited, *Wellington, New Zealand*

Contents

iii

FOREWORD

Children who are impulsive or overactive are difficult to raise, no matter what the cause of these personality characteristics. The needs of a demanding child can lead to problems with lasting impact on the lives of the entire family.

In addressing these problems, play is one of the surest, most potent tools available to children, parents, teachers and other helpers. Playing games is a way of learning and conquering the inevitable hurdles of growing up. It is especially good, strong medicine because it's fun.

It is exciting to see how Dr. Shapiro puts this good medicine to work. He offers us a wealth of practical information, easily used by parents and teachers of children with special problems. There is also much here of value for all adults who have contact with children and the normal problems of childhood.

Dr. Shapiro writes with the same compassion, creativity and sensitivity he has always demonstrated for the children we have known together. His concern has been not only for the child's immediate problems (the ones that have parents and teachers on the ropes), but also for the adult we want this child to become. Therein lies the ultimate test of what we all do as parents and educators, and the reason why this book is important.

Richard Mier, M.D.
Washington, D.C.

ACKNOWLEDGMENTS

I would like to thank many of the staff at the National Children's Center, Inc. for their help and encouragement during the writing of this book, and in particular Liz Loden, Sherry Cramer, and Howard Smith. I would also like to acknowledge the influence of Mrs. Betty Meyer of the Douglas County School System, Colorado, and Dr. Stephen Hodge of the University of Colorado, both of whom encouraged my creativity in working with children.

Preliminary drawings for the artwork were done by Debbie Califia, Sherry Cramer, and Andrea Smith.

v

Understanding the child without self-control

"Steven is a little monster."

"Michael is an obnoxious brat."

"Brenda ought to be tied to her chair."

"Did you know that Alan is hyperactive? He's doped up on drugs from the moment he gets up."

The above commonly heard remarks point up the fact that although children can be cruel in calling names, adults can be devastating.

Parents and teachers are both guilty of name calling, as are psychologists, counselors, pediatricians—everyone who is annoyed by children who do not respect the rules that adults hold so dear. These are the children who do not stay in their seats, who test the limits, who rarely conform. These are the children who try our patience and wear us out. This book has been written to help you to help them.

The active, impulsive child has one of the most common problems of children between the ages of six and thirteen. A 1971 government-sponsored conference conservatively estimated that as many as 3 percent of all elementary-school-age children experience moderate to severe disorder involving self-control (commonly called *hyperactivity* or *hyperkinesis*), which could require the use of stimulant drugs. But, this is only an estimate of the most seriously affected children. When we add children with milder problems—the mischievous ones who are not fond of school and have a talent for doing the wrong things at the wrong time—we are talking about more than 10 percent of children, two or three in every classroom in America. Of the children with this type of

1

problem, 90 percent are boys (which is why I will primarily use masculine pronouns when referring to this type of child).

But, if the problem is so common, why do adults have so little empathy for the child without self-discipline? Perhaps in a country which overeats, overspends, drinks and smokes too much, the impulsive child has become a hyperbole for our inability to set limits on ourselves.

Nearly every adult to whom I've mentioned this book has replied, "Oh, do you have a book like that for people my age?" In a society where individual responsibility is the bottom-line answer to a world gone haywire, self-control is the ultimate virtue.

The problem goes even further. Children without self-control strip away our personal myths that we control our own lives. You think you are in control of your emotions, until one day you find that *you* are the parent people are staring at in the supermarket because you are yelling at your child. Or, you are the teacher who is livid in the lunchroom, because Peter knocked the books off your desk for the third time this week and you lost control and shrieked at the whole class of seven and eight-year-olds. Overactive children make us late, make us tired and cranky, make us want to run away from home. These children are a double threat to our self-image. They seem to mock the very values we hold so dear and simultaneously bring out our own irrational and immature behaviors.

But, you cannot let a child that you wish to help become your adversary. It is difficult to get an enemy to respect you, and harder still to show regard and affection for him.

You can console yourself, however, knowing that research shows that even the most active and uninhibited child will outgrow these behaviors by the time he reaches mid-adolescence, whether he is treated or not. But while life gets easier for *us*, it may be even harder for the child. Well-designed studies have shown that even though the activity level of an overactive child may lessen and level off to normal in adolescence, the social and academic problems that the child has experienced in his early years of schooling may have a profound effect on his adjustment for years to come.

Why My Child?

There are many theories on why children have poor self-control (I prefer to use this phrase because it is less pejorative than the more common labels *hyperactive, hyperkinetic, behaviorally disturbed*), but it is nearly impossible to pinpoint the exact causes in any one child. While many people think that children with severe problems in self-control have abnormal brain-wave patterns, reviews of the research literature suggest

2

that only 1 to 15 percent of children who are labeled hyperkinetic or hyperactive have an organic basis to their problem. Another physiological explanation for why these children behave so unpredictably is that they have specific food allergies, namely to artificial food colors and preservatives, which allegedly set off biochemical reactions and ultimately frenetic behavioral responses. But while there are hundreds of reports of children who turned from devil to angel almost overnight when additives were removed from their diet, the percentage of children who actually respond to this treatment is still not known.

Another school of thought is that overactivity and distractibility are symptomatic reactions to psychological stress, such as anxiety over family problems or fear of failure in school. The psychological approach to the problem of self-control assumes that when an environment lacks a sense of order and structure, children internalize the problems of the adults around them and their behavioral patterns reflect the confusion they cannot articulate. Parents and teachers then unwittingly reinforce these patterns by giving children the most attention when they are disruptive and demanding.

Still another explanation of why children have problems in self-control (and the one that underlies most of the principles in this book) is that they have certain developmental deficits which distinguish them in temperament from their siblings and classmates. Research has suggested that such characteristics as activity level, adaptability, mood, attention span, and persistence may be stable personality traits which are recognizable as early as infancy.

While these theories imply that there are single cause-effect relationships for children with problems in self-control, in practice the majority of impulsive children I have seen appear to have a combination of physiological, psychological, and developmental causes for their behaviors. So, I prefer to turn my attention to deciding how to help children rather than where to place the blame.

Methods Used to Help Impulsive Children

Because there is a wide range of children with problems in self-control, there must be an equally diverse group of treatment strategies. You don't chase after a fly with a sledgehammer, nor do you treat every child who fidgets in his chair with medication. But, because we can rarely pinpoint the precise cause of a child's problem, choosing a treatment is typically a hit-or-miss affair. The rule of thumb, however, is to begin with the

3

approach that will have the least disruptive influence on the child, and to move cautiously along a continuum of greater risk only when there is evidence that the potential benefits offset the potential risks. The remainder of this chapter presents a continuum of treatment methods that I consider when treating a child for problems in self-control. Since there are often extenuating circumstances, however, it is advisable to seek a professional's guidance (usually a pediatrician or psychologist) to help you in your decision.

GAMES TO GROW ON:
THE DEVELOPMENTAL APPROACH

You may think it vain to choose my own book as the basis of the first step to take in helping a child learn self-control, but I must really give the credit to the many researchers and clinicians whose ideas have inspired the games in this book.

The premise of this book is that children with poor self-control lack specific cognitive and behavioral skills which we take for granted in other children of the same age. Skills, as opposed to abilities, can be taught and should follow the general rules of learning. If children have the necessary prerequisite skills, are motivated to learn, and practice the new skills sufficiently, then they should be able to make up or compensate for any deficits they might have in the complex interaction of mind and body that is needed for self-control.

The developmental skills that the child must learn are presented in game format so that they will be fun as well as challenging. The games can be taught and practiced with any adult who has the interest and patience to work with a child with poor self-control. Most of the games can be played in the home or the school without drawing attention to the child as being different or disobedient. All the games have been selected specifically with the impulsive, overactive child in mind, so that there is a diminished chance of the child failing or of the adult becoming so frustrated as to be unable to work effectively with the child. Most of the games can be played in 5 or 10 minutes (the average attention span for the impulsive child) and yet they are interesting enough so the child will want to play them over and over again—practicing new skills and learning new controls. These games will be most effective, however, when you follow the principle discussed in Chapter 3.

THE PSYCHOTHERAPEUTIC APPROACH

Some form of psychotherapy is often indicated for children with problems in self-control. However, parents are rarely aware of the range of psychological services that are available to them, or of how to evaluate these services. I offer the following suggestions in the hope that parents will become more educated and discriminating consumers before they make a large emotional and financial investment.

Seek out a psychologist or psychiatrist who is experienced in working with impulsive children. Don't be afraid to ask, "How many children have you treated who are like my child? How do things usually work out?" There are many myths and misconceptions about impulsive children, and professionals are not immune to them. The more experienced professional will usually have developed the patience, the imagination, and the perseverance necessary to work successfully with active-impulsive children.

Ask the clinician how he or she intends to work with the child. The most common approach is a holistic one: the whole child and his environment are looked at, not just the immediate problem. Commonly, the psychotherapeutic plan will include working with the child's teacher(s) as well as with his family. I am personally wary of recommending a colleague who only works with the child alone in his or her office at a fixed hour and day of the week. This approach is fine for adults, but the key to working with children is communication, and this takes a flexible professional who is not entirely office-bound.

It is reasonable to ask the therapist how long he or she thinks the child (or family) will need therapy, and just what the total costs will be. Some therapists will enter into a form of contract with the parents which will state just what they will do, for how long, and what they hope the final outcome will be. While not every therapist will be this specific, the general trend in psychological services is to de-mystify the therapeutic process, and to involve the parent and the child in a working alliance.

Consider whether the therapist who works with the child has other professionals to consult with, notably a pediatrician, nutritionist, neurologist, psychiatrist, or educational specialist. Although these extra professionals are usually only needed in the more complex cases, the interdisciplinary approach to treating children is becoming increasingly popular. The psychotherapist, however, should take the primary responsibility for pulling the information together for you, and you should be confident that he or she is willing to take on this task.

Finally, you should be aware that seeking psychological help for your child need not be a long-drawn-out and expensive undertaking. There are many instances in which a few consultations with an experienced therapist may be all that is needed.

THE DIETARY APPROACH

Another low-risk approach to treating the overactive child is to modify the child's diet. There appear to be many children who are allergic to food coloring, preservatives, and certain other substances, but instead of

5

triggering a rash or respiratory reaction, their allergies make them distract-ible, create short attention spans, and cause bursts of uncontrollable energy.

Although there are no conclusive studies to tell us just how many children have behavior problems as a result of food allergies, there are so many dramatic case studies in which children seemed to have new personalities when their diet was changed, that we cannot rule out the potential of this approach. On the other hand, changing the eating habits of a child (and usually of the rest of the family too) is not an easy matter, and occasionally may even have adverse effects if the child is not getting sound nutrition.

The diets usually prescribed for overactive children emphasize eating natural foods without artificial colors or preservatives. In addition, most diets eliminate white and brown sugar and advise that even the use of honey to be kept to a minimum. Allergists may also recommend that certain foods (such as almonds, cherries, grapes, and apples, which contain natural salicylates) be removed from a child's diet for a specific period of time.

There are a few nonmedical drawbacks to the dietary approach, which although they do not involve risks to the child, may nevertheless undermine your efforts. First is the inconvenience and expense of this program. To successfully provide a natural diet for a youngster, you must change the buying, cooking, and eating habits of the whole family. No more fast foods. No more candy and other treats around the house. More time spent in buying and preparing foods without additives and perserva-tives. Family members may begin to resent this. The child may start to "cheat," and in sympathy you may begin to allow sugars and processed foods on special occasions. Before you know it, you're back to the same eating patterns as before, and you think, "This diet didn't help at all," but you really haven't given it a chance.

If you have ever been on a diet yourself, you know how hard it is to change old eating patterns, and how easy it is to rationalize your slipups. To overcome these natural difficulties you may wish to seek support from other families who have gone through the same process. The Feingold Society (P.O. Box 18116, Washington, D.C. 20011) is a nonprofit organization which promotes dietary management for children with be-havior disorders, and can put you in touch with families having similar problems and concerns.

THE EDUCATIONAL APPROACH

Treating the child with poor self-control from an educational standpoint typically involves modifications in the child's regular class, arrangements to use a learning resource room, or placement in a special classroom for children with behavioral problems. As a result of recent federal legislation

(Public Law 94-142, the Education for all Handicapped Children's Act), special programs for children with problems are now available throughout the country. To be enrolled in any special program, however, the child must first be diagnosed by a psychologist, usually one employed by the school system, as having a significant emotional-behavioral problem which inhibits learning in a traditional classroom setting. Once this assessment has been made, the parents and the teachers, testers, and other school personnel are called into a conference and the various educational strategies offered by the school system (including placement in special private schools) are discussed. Most often, children are worked with within their regular classroom (this is called *mainstreaming*). However, if the child's problems are severe, this may be impossible, and he/she may be enrolled in a special class, usually with eight to ten children with similar problems, for all or part of the school day. While there is no financial cost when a child is placed in a special classroom, there is an emotional cost for both the parent and the child. This cost has to do with the labeling of the child as "different" from his peers and with his segregation from children without problems. For some children, placement in a special classroom can aggravate the problems they already have. The child may resent being thought of as "crazy" or "weird" and he may express this resentment by acting up even more. He may develop an even poorer self-image if other children tease him about his needs, or worst of all, he may learn more maladaptive behaviors by imitating other children with more severe problems.

But don't let me scare you too much. In all types of treatments there is some degree of risk, but the concerned adults must ask themselves: Do the gains outweight the risks involved? Thousands of children are helped by special classes throughout the country each year, and many of them return to a normal classroom setting. However, special programs vary considerably, and the nonprofessional rarely has the expertise or opportunity to evaluate the program before the child is placed. This is not right. Because the child cannot make the decision himself, you must be his advocate, and you must feel that you are capable of making an informed decision before you do anything.

Don't agree to placing your child in a special program before you have seen it in operation. You must do more than just meet with the child's new teacher; you should ask to see the class as it normally operates. Do the other children remind you of your own child, or do they seem to have many more problems? Are the children working and learning? This is the purpose of schooling, and you should accept no less. Here is a list of some specific things to look for and ask about. These items describe a model classroom for a child with severe problems in self-control. If school personnel feel that your child can benefit from special classroom placement, go through this checklist with the teacher or principal. These are educational variables that research studies have shown to be most effective in providing educational alternatives to children with problems in self-control, and if you cannot check off at least half of the eight items, then I would judge this program to be unacceptable for a child with such problems.

★ There should be separate study areas in the room for each child with poor self-control. These children are typically easily distracted, and a study carrel (or similar visual boundary) will help him to keep his mind on his work.

★ Pencils, papers, crayons, books, and similar items should *not* be kept at the child's desk but should be in an area at least ten feet away. These are additional distractions for the child and are frequently a source of confrontation between the child and the teacher.

★ Work times in the class should be highly structured, consistent, and realistic. The child must have a work schedule which is at a reasonable level of expectation, and which is the same each day. If a child can only work for five minutes at a time, then it is unreasonable to expect him to work for one-half hour at a time, but he should have frequent short work periods throughout the day, and the length of these periods should be gradually increased as he becomes more familiar with the work.

★ The work should always be interesting. Everyone works harder and longer when the work is fun. This takes a creative and imaginative teacher.

★ Male teachers are generally preferable to female teachers for a class of children with problems in self-control. Research has shown that most males have a higher tolerance for the boisterous and rowdy activity that is typical of these children, and this helps give the child the message: I understand your need for activity, I like it too. But you can be like me and learn when to play and when to work.

★ Because children without self-control often have other learning problems as well, instruction must be systematic. The teacher must at all times know what objectives he or she has for each child in each learning area and how to move the child toward these objectives by following a sequence of ordered tasks. A child should not be allowed to skip over basic skills merely because the rest of the class has completed a unit. If a child cannot multiply, he must learn to do so before he goes on to division. The child's learning program must be tailored so that it suits his individual needs.

★ Children must be encouraged to learn in all areas where they will meet with success, not just in the traditional academic subjects. Creative arts therapists have specific training in helping children with problems

8

using dance, art, and music. These professionals should be available to every program set up for children with problems.

If your child receives special educational services in your school system, federal law mandates that an *individual education plan* be written for each child and that this plan be discussed with the child's parents. The individual education plan (called IEP) should stipulate most of the points that I have mentioned and should give you a reasonably clear idea as to what the teacher plans to do or not do. If you find the language of the plan confusing, or if you feel that the plan is not being followed or is not adequate, there are grievance procedures, which are also mandated by law, that you should follow to ensure that your child is getting the best education possible. You also may wish to contact professional educators who are independent of the school system, or other parents who have been through similar circumstances. The largest organization for children with special needs is The Council for Exceptional Children (1920 Association Drive, Reston, Virginia 22091). Its toll-free number is (800) 336-3728, and it can frequently put you in touch with people in your locality who can give you sound educational advice.

MEDICAL INTERVENTION

I have placed medical intervention at the end of the continuum because although medication can be highly effective in helping a child, the risks can also be substantial. After decades of prescriptions for children with poor self-control, the medical establishment is only now beginning to realize what the side effects of stimulant drugs can be: loss of appetite, loss of sleep, cardiovascular problems, the stigma of being a drug user, a psychological addiction to the drug.

So medication should be used cautiously and conservatively. It should never be the only approach to a child's problem but should be used in conjunction with sound educational and behavioral management programs. Physical examinations should be frequent throughout the period the child is on medication in order to detect the subtlest of side effects. The effects of the drug must be followed closely and should be reported frequently to the physician. Physicians should not have to rely on anecdotal or subjective information to evaluate the effectiveness of the drug, but plans should be made in advance of the treatment to measure objectively the proposed effect of the medication. You should minimally measure at least one behavior that should increase (for example, ability to stay seated) and a second behavior that should decrease (for example, distractibility).

Finally, each child receiving medication for behavioral problems should periodically take a "drug vacation." This is to see if the child can maintain his level of functioning without the medication, as well as to see

9

just what role the drugs have in keeping the child on the road to learning. Parents and teachers should always follow the physician's orders in administering medication. Too frequently parents take it upon themselves to give or withhold a child's medication as they see fit, depending on how the child is behaving at a given time. Most parents who do this are trying to get the child off the medication whenever possible (for example, weekends or long vacations), but to do this without specific instructions from a physician is extremely ill advised. While the intentions of these parents are good, such a policy might undermine the entire program that has been designed for the child. If you are uneasy about your physician's approach to medication, get a second medical opinion from a physician you respect instead of taking it on yourself to play doctor.

Disciplining the child who lacks self-control: changing old habits

When a child comes to me who by the age of five or six has little or no self-control, I automatically assume that the parents have a problem in disciplining the child. Problems in self-control are always related to problems that parents have in disciplining, even though, as with the chicken and the egg, we never really know which comes first.

There are generally two paths that lead to a discipline problem—either the child is born with a personality that is mismatched to his parents' natural style of disciplining, or there are basic conflicts within the family that make the parents' method of disciplining cause more problems than it solves.

Let's look at the problem of mismatching first. As discussed in the previous chapter, there are genetic, psychological, and developmental reasons why some children are harder to discipline than others. A couple's first child may have been a quiet little boy—almost placid, like his parents—who liked to play by himself. But for no apparent reason, their second child is demanding and temperamental from as early an age as anyone can remember. While the first child—let's call him Stephen—responded immediately to a raised eyebrow or the slightest voice inflection, the second boy—let's call him Benjamin—seems completely insensitve to his parents' wishes. He constantly pushes them to their limit. He does poorly in school although he seems to be bright. He talks back to adults, plays hookey, steals, lies frequently, keeps secrets to himself. Neither parent was like this when young.

While the parents took disciplining for granted with their older son, they are at a loss what to do with Benjamin. They send him to his room, but he doesn't seem to mind. They take away his allowance, and he steals what he wants. If they spank him, he holds back his tears in resentment, and sometimes won't talk to anyone for days. Then the mood lifts, he is back to normal, with the same problems. Whatever Benjamin's parents try, nothing seems to work. They feel that they are getting stricter and stricter with their younger son, and he seems to need punishment every day. Both parents feel helpless, and sometimes hopeless. Each one thinks, "One day I'm going to get a one-way ticket and not look back," but they can't talk about this, even to each other.

In Benjamin's family no one is really at fault. His problem is largely one of disposition. He is active and excitable while everyone else in the family is quiet and even-tempered. Although his parents love him and try everything that makes sense to control him, Benjamin has become a stranger in his own home, a time bomb which explodes every day in yet another family crisis.

Parents are most likely to use the same type of discipline on their children as they themselves received. This is what they are comfortable with, because it is familiar. Benjamin's parents were both easy to raise. They weren't disciplined very much—they didn't need to be. So when Benjamin came along, they had a very small repertoire of disciplining techniques. Benjamin needed more structure and more discipline than either they or their first son, but by the time they realized it, they did too little too late. More important, they were not confident about what they did. When they sent Benjamin to his room without supper, they felt so guilty that they brought him a special meal at the end of the evening. When Benjamin's father spanked him for stealing or lying, his mother felt so badly that she hurt more than her son, and the father came to feel that spanking meant punishing not only his son but his wife too. These are examples of what I mean by a disciplining mismatch. One or both parents are simply not equipped to provide the type of discipline that their child needs, and although they go through all the right attempts at disciplining, there is a natural conflict between what they *have* to do and what they *want* to do. Their hearts simply aren't in it, and so one or both parents undermine even their most sincere attempts. When they come into my office, and I ask them, "How do you punish your child?" everything they say seems right. Except for the fact that nothing works, and Benjamin has not learned self-control.

But let's look at another family, that of Brenda, whose problems in self-control came later in her life, at about the time she entered school. Brenda's early childhood was fairly typical. She talked early and walked late. She went through the same stages as most other children, and was sometimes better behaved than others.

12

Her parents were also pretty typical. Both parents worked, and although they loved their daughter, they did not always take the time to talk to her and understand her point of view, but then neither did they talk too much to each other. Both parents were under a lot of stress at their jobs, and frequently they were tired and irritable in the evenings and even on the weekends. When they were asked, "Just how do you discipline Brenda?" they really couldn't say. She had never been a problem until recently. Whatever they did seemed to work. So I asked for some examples.

Brenda's mother began. "The only time I can remember hitting Brenda was when she was four. She liked to play ball in the house, in the living room, while I cooked dinner. I'd tell her to stop it, and she usually did, but then the next day she'd do it again. Then one night, I remember I was really tired because I had worked a ten-hour shift. Brenda was playing with her ball in the living room, even though she knew better. I was setting out the dishes, when I heard this crash, and when I went in, my best vase was broken. I was furious at her, so I took down her pants then and there, and spanked her on the bottom. Then I sent her to her room, and she missed her dinner."

"So what did Brenda learn from this?" I asked.

"Well, she never played ball in the house again. And I don't think I ever spanked her again either. Well, maybe once."

But perhaps Brenda learned more than her mother realized. At the age of four she learned that adults are unpredictable. When they say no it doesn't really mean anything, until you break or hurt something of theirs. Then all hell breaks loose.

Then I turned to Brenda's father and asked him for an example of how he disciplines his daughter. "Well, I'll tell you something I do now," he began. "It's about her school work, which I guess is why we're really here. Brenda's a smart girl, and I expect her to make good grades. Her teacher sends home her tests every Friday, and if I see any grade lower than a B, then I don't give her any allowance for that week. Brenda doesn't like that, because then she can't go out with the other kids in the neighborhood and see movies and buy ice cream and stuff. That worked fine in first grade, but this year, nothing works. Her teacher says she doesn't try, she goofs off, she's disrespectful, and I don't know what. It's a mess now."

"Tell me, what happens when Brenda brings home A's?"

Brenda's mother replied, "Oh, I make a big fuss," but her father said, "Why, I say, 'That's good, that's what I expect.' "

So what did Brenda learn from this type of disciplining? She learned that her mistakes will not be tolerated. That if she brings home bad grades, not only will she meet with disapproval from her parents, but indirectly she will meet with disapproval from her friends because she will

13

not have the money to participate in their weekend activities. She learned that life is unfair in terms of rewards and punishments, at least in terms of her schoolwork, for even one C brings on a fairly severe punishment, while B's and even A's do not bring on any equal rewards. She also has learned that she must really excel to get praise from her mother, but even then her father is emotionally detached, for he has very high, possibly unrealistic expectations.

Now, let us look, just from these two incidents, at what Brenda has not learned.

She did not learn consideration, or empathy, from the incident in which she broke the vase with the ball. If she had learned this, she wouldn't have kept playing ball when her mother said not to; she stopped only because she feared another spanking. Nor did she learn to do well in school from her father's punishment of her poor grades. Moreover, she did not learn good study and work habits, nor to take pride in her achievements.

For different reasons, both Benjamin and Brenda have problems in self-control. For different reasons, they both have not learned the skills of self-discipline that they will need to succeed outside of the family. While under the premise of this book, they can be taught these skills by an involved and empathic adult, their parents and teachers will continue to be confused about how to handle their problems. Unless instructed to do otherwise, they will continue the same habits and reactions they have unwittingly contributed to the problems of these children.

Benjamin and Brenda cannot change their behaviors in a vacuum. If they are to learn new ways to control themselves, their parents and teachers, and even grandparents, older siblings, baby-sitters—all significant adults in their lives—must reexamine their approach to discipline. Changing their patterns will be difficult, but it will be well worth the effort.

GAMES TO LEARN NEW DISCIPLINING HABITS

There have been many books and articles written on new disciplining techniques, most of which work if they are used conscientiously and consistently. However, this is rarely the case. As I have pointed out, an adult's style of discipline is primarily a result of that adult's own upbringing and is enmeshed in his or her personality and most basic behaviors. This makes it difficult to change. We might say that an adult's style of disciplining is a *habit*—a behavior which is related to basic unconscious needs and repeated so often that it is automatic.

14

So if you think you're ready to change your pattern of disciplining a child with problems in self-control, first think about the successes and failures you have had in changing your other habits—overeating, smoking, drinking, nail-biting, hair pulling, talking too much, nervous mannerisms, and so forth. To change a habit, you need self-control yourself, the very thing that you want to teach the child. If you are like most adults, you have had a hard time changing your habits, and yet if your desire is strong enough, and you have some techniques to help you, it can be done.

The following six games, or exercises, will teach you to develop the new habits you will need if you are to effectively discipline a child without self-control. Try them all before you begin working with the child, and have other adults who discipline the child try them as well. They will help you begin to change your patterns of behavior. They will help you realize some of your own strengths and weaknesses in self-control. And hopefully they will help you empathize with the child you are trying to work with and the problems the child must surmount. I want you to play each game twice, once to learn about your own personal habits that you don't like, and a second time to learn about your disciplining habits that may be a problem to the child whom you really want to help.

You can win up to 140 points by playing all the games in this chapter; 140 being a perfect score. As an incentive to play and to learn to change your discipline habits, you should set aside some money and pay yourself 50 cents for every point that you win. Anything over 90 points is an excellent score. Isn't there something for $45 that you'd like to have for yourself but you haven't gotten? Some clothing? A special night out? A luxury you would normally deny yourself? As we shall see in Chapter 3, motivation is an important part of learning and changing through games, so reward yourself for games well played and new habits well learned.

targets

The first habit I want you to break is thinking that the child with problems in self-control is all bad. He's not. He has some behaviors that are very serious problems for himself and for others, and other behaviors which are really not that serious but are just annoying. And like everyone, the child does many things that are endearing and lovable. However, you may be too frustrated and concerned to think about these very often. To really help the child you must learn to see the entire range of his behaviors and to give priority to the ones that are most serious. A basic

15

tenet of behavioral psychology is that you can only change one behavior at a time, so it makes sense to start with the one that is important.

Figure 1 shows two targets. Target A has a list of habits common to adults and Target B has a list of problems common to children. Begin this game by looking at the habits around Target A, and circle all the ones that you have. List any additional habits not mentioned in the space provided. Now write in your least important habits in the outer rings of the target, and write in the habits that are most important to you closer to the center. Put your single most important habit—the one that you would most like to change—in the bull's-eye. This is your target behavior, a change which receives top priority.

Figure 1

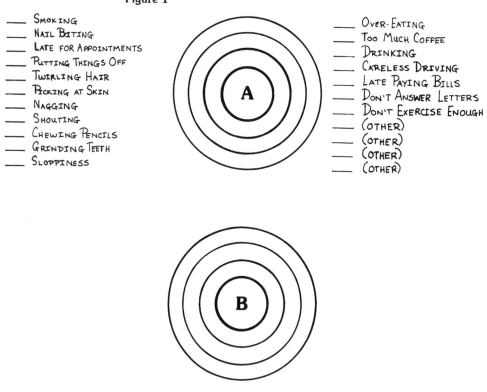

_____ SMOKING
_____ NAIL BITING
_____ LATE FOR APPOINTMENTS
_____ PUTTING THINGS OFF
_____ TWIRLING HAIR
_____ PICKING AT SKIN
_____ NAGGING
_____ SHOUTING
_____ CHEWING PENCILS
_____ GRINDING TEETH
_____ SLOPPINESS

_____ OVER-EATING
_____ TOO MUCH COFFEE
_____ DRINKING
_____ CARELESS DRIVING
_____ LATE PAYING BILLS
_____ DON'T ANSWER LETTERS
_____ DON'T EXERCISE ENOUGH
_____ (OTHER)
_____ (OTHER)
_____ (OTHER)
_____ (OTHER)

_____ HITS OTHER CHILDREN
_____ TELLS LIES
_____ TAKES THINGS THAT BELONG TO OTHERS
_____ CAN'T STAY SEATED
_____ WON'T FOLLOW DIRECTIONS
_____ POOR STUDY HABITS
_____ DOESN'T CLEAN UP AFTER SELF

_____ DISTRACTIBLE
_____ SHORT ATTENTION SPAN
_____ DISRESPECTFUL
_____ (OTHER)_____
_____ (OTHER)_____
_____ (OTHER)_____
_____ (OTHER)_____

16

You may notice that some other habits are so similar that they are just different ways of saying the same thing. For instance, the person who is a nail biter, pencil chewer, and teeth grinder is really showing different forms of the same habit, and it may be advantageous to try to change all three things at once rather than to think of them as unrelated behaviors.

Now fill in target B for the child you intend to work with, first circling the behaviors that best characterize the child and adding any others that you think are important. Again put the behaviors you are least concerned about in the outer rings of the target and the more significant behaviors (to the child) toward the center. Write the one behavior that is most important in the bull's-eye. Just as with your own habits, you may notice that some terms used to characterize behaviors are just different ways of saying the same thing; for example, distractibility, short attention span, and lack of concentration. Although they are not really synonomous, these three behavioral traits form a cluster that is so interbound that it can be treated as one target behavior.

To score this game, show target B to another adult concerned with the same child's problems. Explain the principle behind the target: that the behaviors are rated as to their relative importance by their distance from the bull's eye. Have the other adult put an arrow alongside any behaviors that he or she does not feel are correctly placed on the target. The arrow should point toward the bull's-eye if the other adult thinks the behavior is more important and away from the bull's-eye if he or she thinks the behavior is less important in relation to the child's growth and development. Discuss the proposed changes. Give yourself five points for each behavior, that, after the discussion, you think you had originally placed correctly on the target. Give yourself ten bonus points if the adult agrees with you on the one behavior you have placed in the bull's-eye. This is the most important behavior I want you to think about now as we turn to the next game. And continue to practice:

Habit #1: Stop thinking of your child as all bad. Realize that some of his problems are more serious to his growth than others, and put your time and energy into helping him with these problems first.

clues and cues

When adults are around children with problems in self-control, they are often less logical than they are in other situations. This is because they are always reacting to the child's problem rather than having the child learn to react to them. And the nature of the type of child we are talking about is to be unpredictable and erratic, so that the adults around

17

such children typically feel as if they were caught in a whirlwind. I want you to break the habit of thinking that these children are beyond your reason and logic. This isn't true. The second step in learning to discipline a child with problems in self-control is to look for the clues that can forewarn you that your child will be repeating a behavior you don't like and to try to catch the problem before it occurs. In psychological terms, these clues are called *antecedents*.

Remember Benjamin, the boy we talked about earlier in this chapter, who tested his parents' patience since he was an infant? His mother and father played the preceding TARGETS game and pinpointed his stealing as his most serious behavior problem. So I asked them to look at the clues which Benjamin gave them just before he was about to take something. To help them do this I had them play a game of CLUES AND CUES.

To begin the game, the parents had to write down answers to the following questions:

1. How often does he steal? How many times per day? Per week?
2. What does he steal?
3. When does he steal? What days? What times of the day?
4. Where does he steal? At home? At school? From stores?
5. What is he like before he steals? Happy? Angry?
6. Are there other things that Benjamin does just before he steals? Other problems or maybe even good things?
7. Are there specific events that seem to occur just before he steals? Such as his brother coming home with good marks from school, or his parents spending an unusual amount of time away from home?

When Benjamin's parents had answered these questions, I asked them to compare their answers and to look for a pattern in their son's behavior.

There is always a pattern to human behavior, although we don't always see it. When we can identify the pattern of a child with problems by the clues he gives us, then we can begin to help the child by breaking his cycle of misbehavior, punishment, bad feelings, and more misbehavior.

However it is not really enough just to rely on your memory. When we looked at Benjamin's parents' answers, there was a lot of disagreement. His mother emphasized one clue and his father another. So what was the truth? It was easy to find out. Benjamin's parents only had to observe and record the behavior that they had targeted, the stealing, to see the nature of the problem and when and where it occurred. They did this by filling out a weekly chart (see Fig. 2). When this chart is filled out conscientiously a pattern will emerge and *clues* become *cues*, which will tell adults interested in helping the child when the target behavior is about

18

Figure 2 CUES CHART

Instructions: Record the habit you targeted for yourself and the problem you have targeted for the child on separate sheets. Be as conscientious as you can in recording every time the behaviors occur.

	Monday	Tuesday	Wednesday	Thursday	Friday	Saturday	Sunday
Target behavior							
Time							
Place							
What Happened Before?							
Target behavior							
Time							
Place							
What Happened Before?							
Target behavior							
Time							
Place							
What Happened Before?							
Target behavior							
Time							
Place							
What Happened Before?							
Target behavior							
Time							
Place							
What Happened Before?							
Target behavior							
Time							
Place							
What Happened Before?							
Target behavior							
Time							
Place							
What Happened Before?							
Target behavior							
Time							
Place							
What Happened Before?							

to occur. Armed with this knowledge, sometimes an entire discipline problem can be eliminated.

To play CLUES AND CUES, you should first practice looking for patterns in your own habit, the one that you have identified in the first game. Answer the same questions that I asked Benjamin's parents: How often does the problem occur? What does it consist of? When does it happen? Where does it happen? What do you feel or do just before it happens? What specific events take place just before it happens? Write down the answers to these questions.

Now see how accurate you are by recording your behaviors on a copy of Fig. 2 for a whole week. Do you see a pattern of cues? Have you learned to anticipate your habit? Repeat the game for the child you are working with, first answering the same questions about the problem you have targeted, and then recording the problem's occurrence for a whole week (you can do this simultaneously as you record your own habits if you wish). Sometimes you might find that a problem does not occur that often, so that you must record the behavior for more than a week, but then you should reconsider whether it is really the most important problem to work on at this time.

To score this game, give yourself one point for each clue that you have identified in learning about your own as well as the child's behavior. Some examples of cues are: "I play with my hair when I'm nervous. I smoke more during the week than on weekends. The child has more problems in class at the beginning of the week than at the end." These predictive statements are made by examining the behavioral chart and noting when and where the behaviors occur most frequently; the types of things that take place in the environment before the problem occurs; and the child's mood before the problem occurs.

Here is the habit I want you to get into:

Habit #2: Look for cues that tell you that a child is about to misbehave. Try to catch the problem before it starts.

relax about things

Now I have an easy game for you. Sit down in a comfortable chair. Turn down the lights. Relax yourself. Relax the muscles in your arms, your legs, your feet, your fingers, your face. Breathe deeply and quietly. Now I want you to think about the habit you are trying to control. Get a mental image of yourself doing it. Is it smoking? Then see yourself in the environment where you smoke the most. Picture yourself lighting up a cigarette (don't do it—just think about it). See yourself drawing the

20

smoke in and then exhaling it. Now relax again. Breathe deeply, and let your muscles loosen all over your body. Now think about the problem behavior that you are working on with your child. See him doing it in your mind. Is it running around the house? Visualize the room he is in. What is he doing and saying? Now put yourself in the picture. See yourself watching him, in the same room. Breathe deeply and relax as you imagine this. Relax all your muscles again. Let the weight of your arms go, and your shoulders. Now get one more mental picture. Something very tranquil, such as a beach, or yourself at the ocean. Let your mind go and your body relax. Keep breathing deeply until you are ready to get up. Do you feel refreshed?

Now I want to tell you the purpose of this game. I want you to get into the habit of relaxing about the problem you want to control in yourself and about the discipline problems that you are having with the child. To break your old habits, you must break into your response pattern, which is physical as well as emotional. When you see your child is misbehaving, this triggers an emotional reaction and your body chemistry begins to change. Your blood pressure may rise, your body produces more adrenalin, and your heart beats faster. This is a stress reaction, and it prevents you from reacting calmly and logically to the child's problem or your own habits (for more details about this technique read *The Relaxation Response,* by Herbert Benson, listed in the Suggested Reading section).

Practice this game at least ten times, and give yourself two points each time you practice it.

Now the next time you discipline your child, I want you to relax before you do or say anything. Breathe deeply for 30 seconds. Relax your muscles; don't tighten them. Clear your mind and think of the tranquil scene you had imagined in your chair, sitting on the beach or lying in a cloud. Here's the habit I want you to get into:

Habit #3: Relax until you are calm before you discipline your child. You will not be able to help him learn self-control if you can't control your own feelings first.

mirror, mirror on the wall

Do you remember the fairy tale "Snow White" and particularly part where the queen looks into the mirror and asks, "Who is the fairest of them all?" This is what I want you to do in this game—to look at a reflection of yourself and to learn to be a reflection for the child that you want to help. When you do this, however, you will use a different

21

meaning of the word "fairest" than the one in the fairy tale. You will reflect a second meaning of the word when you have to discipline: impartial, just and honest, unprejudiced.

The first thing you must do to develop this new habit is to stop using punishments as a way to criticize your child. When you do this you say in one way or another "You are bad—I dislike you," and the child readily believes this about himself. He incorporates this message into his self-image so that at some point he says to himself, "I don't really need to control myself because everyone thinks I'm bad anyway." And so the child who has difficulty in self-control now has an excuse for his behavior.

The purpose of punishing or disciplining a child is not to make him feel badly about himself, but to change his behaviors so that he can have a good self-image. If we humiliate, embarrass, or otherwise demean the child, then we are defeating our own purposes.

Instead of criticizing a child as you punish him, you must help him learn why he is being punished by being a mirror to the child, sensitively reflecting to him what has occurred. There are some simple techniques that you can use to do this. First, remain calm. If you have played the previous game, then you should be able to do this without too much trouble. You must remain calm even when there is paint on the walls, glass in the carpet, and paper shreds in every corner.

Next, you should stop asking the child "why" questions. Every adult wants to know the answer to why a child does something wrong, but have you ever heard a child with problems in self-control answer this question? Of course not. So stop asking it. It only frustrates the child and you. Instead, help the child to learn about his own actions and feelings by reflecting what you see. Children often cannot express themselves in words, so they use actions instead. So you must set an example of how to reverse this process by *putting actions into words*. Describe to the child what has happened. Describe to him what you think he is feeling, and what you are feeling. Help clarify the events surrounding the problem.

For an example, let's take a look at Benjamin's stealing again. His mother finds that a dollar bill is missing from her dresser. She is very sure that Benjamin took it because he is the only one in the house and she just saw it. She knows that her son wants money to buy himself some candy. She once might have said, in anger, "Benjamin, did you take my money? I know you did. Give it back to me now! What's the matter with you? I can't trust you for a minute." But now she describes and clarifies: "Benjamin, there was a dollar on my dresser. You and I are the only ones in the house. I saw it there just five minutes ago. I'm going to have to punish you for taking it."

Benjamin doesn't respond.

His mother says, "You don't want to talk about it?" (She is describing his reaction).

Benjamin says, "I didn't do it."

MOTHER: You don't want to say that you took the money. (She accepts what he says and just restates it.)

BENJAMIN: I never have money of my own.

MOTHER: You don't think you have any way to get money on your own?

BENJAMIN: Everyone else has a job but me.

MOTHER: Do you want to make money by performing jobs for me? I think that we can arrange that. (She changes the negative behavior into a positive one. We will see more of how to do this in the next game.)

(Benjamin is quiet. He shuffles his feet and looks restless.)

MOTHER: You're mad at me because you know I'm going to punish you. (She describes the feeling she thinks he must have. He will correct her if she is wrong.)

BENJAMIN: No, I'm not mad. I didn't do anything.

MOTHER: When you're quiet like this, and you shuffle your feet, that usually means you're mad or upset. I got mad too when I saw my dollar was missing. (She is helping him learn how behaviors can show your feelings by saying that she gets mad too.)

BENJAMIN: If I pay you the money back next week, do I have to get punished?

MOTHER: Yes. That is what we have agreed on. (She reflects the reality of the situation.) But you can earn a dollar later by raking leaves.

You will notice from this dialogue that Benjamin's mother did not back down from disciplining her child. She knew that a punishment would eventually come and helping Benjamin understand what had happened did not keep her from showing him the consequences of his stealing. Being fair with a child is not synonymous with being lenient.

Now I want you to get in front of a mirror and practice this type of dialogue with yourself. Start with your own habit that you want to control. Talk to yourself about it. Describe the last time you indulged in the habit to yourself. Clarify what you felt and what happened.

I suspect that you've talked to yourself in the mirror before, as might a man who overate until his stomach hurt and who then looked at himself and said, "What a pig you are! You know you didn't want to eat two pieces of cake, but you had them anyway. Another day, another pound."

However this type of self-dialogue is all wrong. It is self-mocking rather than serious. And as you might have guessed, it doesn't keep a person from eating just as much the next time.

Instead, talk to yourself as if you are two people: one being honest and open and the other reflecting, clarifying, describing, and noncritical.

23

For example:

You 1: I ate two pieces of cake. I feel sick to my stomach and guilty. I'm supposed to be on a diet.

You 2: You ate what you didn't want to.

You 1: I sure did. I knew I'd feel like this too.

You 2: You knew you'd feel guilty afterwards, but you couldn't help yourself.

You 1: I always do this.

You 2: A real pattern.

You 1: Yeah. Boy, I need to break this habit.

Now practice one more time in the mirror, thinking about the problem behavior that you have targeted for the child. Play both parts, yours and his. Listen to your voice. Watch your facial expressions. Can you be noncritical and reflective? Are you the fairest of them all? Give yourself one point for every minute that you practice this game, up to 25 points. And practice the following habit as much as you can:

Habit #4: Don't criticize when you punish, but rather reflect to the child what has happened by describing and clarifying to him what he has done and what he is feeling.

let the punishment
overfit the crime

The previous games have all led up to this important question: What do I do for a punishment, if nothing else works? This game will teach you what kind of discipline is most effective and appropriate for the child with problems in self-control. As I have emphasized, correct discipline should be a learning experience for the child, but the child will not be able to learn if he is feeling embarrassed, ashamed, or humiliated. Therefore you must give up some of the more traditional punishments you have tried, such as yelling at the child, spanking him, or sending him to his room without supper (I am assuming that if you are reading this section, these punishments have not worked anyway).

Instead, I want you to learn to use punishments that not only correct the problem that the child has had, but, as the title of this game implies, I want you to have the child overcorrect the problem.

Overcorrection is a powerful behavior modification technique developed by Azrin and Foxx as part of their toilet training program for retarded children, which has proved successful with many different prob-

24

lem behaviors of children. Of the many ways of disciplining a child, I recommend this technique most frequently because it combines many basic psychological principles and it is consistent with the theme of this book: Children can be *instructed* in self-control.

There are two basic steps to the overcorrection method of disciplining. The first is called *restitutional correction* and is aimed at not only restoring things to the way they were, but making them even better than before the problem behavior occurred. For instance, let's say a child throws his clothes all over the floor in a tantrum. Not only will he be required to put away all the clothes he had thrown, but he will have to go further and put away clothes that might belong to someone else in the family.

As you see, the discipline does not provide a balance between the "crime" and "punishment," but rather an exaggeration of what is necessary to make things right. If the child were only required to hang up his own clothes, then this would not be a punishment, for it is only what we expected of him in the first place.

The second step of the overcorrection process is called *positive practice*. In this step, the child is instructed in an appropriate behavior which is a substitute for the inappropriate one he has shown. In the example of the child who has thrown his clothes all over the place, the punishment would include practicing the correct behavior, which is folding and hanging up clothes properly, for a designated number of times.

If it is not obvious, let me emphasize that in both these steps an adult must be present at all times to encourage and guide the child towards the correct behavior and to model a good attitude (we will discuss this more in the next game in the chapter).

But let's look at another example, the overcorrection procedure that Azrin and Foxx recommend in their 24-hour toilet training program. If a child has an accident and soils his clothes, he is required to take them off himself, to clean up any mess, to wash out his clothes, and to put them away. This is the restitutional correction step. He would then be immediately required to go to the place where the accident occurred, go to the toilet, pull down his pants, sit, and pull up his pants, all of which is the behavior he should have practiced in the first place when he felt the urge to relieve himself. This positive practice step is repeated ten times.

In the case of a young or a reluctant child, "guidance" may mean having to physically guide the child's hands through the correct motions; however, it should not mean struggling or wrestling with the child.

The overcorrection technique is not pleasant, but when it is done right, it is fair. It does not humiliate or embarrass the child. Moreover, it is instructive, for it teaches the child that he is responsible for his own

25

actions, and that if he does something wrong, he will have to make it right again. And it gives him the opportunity to learn and practice the correct thing to do.

Now we'll play a matching game to see if you understand the concepts behind this technique. I want you to match the correct two steps of the overcorrection method (restitutional correction and positive practice) listed in column B to the correct problem behavior listed in column A. You can find the answers to this game in Appendix B. You get one point for each correct answer.

*A—Sample Behavioral
Problems*

*B—Overcorrection
Techniques*

1. Jamie neglects his chores
   _____(restitutional correction)
   _____(positive practice)
2. Jamie hits children at school.
   _____(restitutional correction)
   _____(positive practice)
3. Jamie steals toys from his younger sister and breaks them.
   _____(restitutional correction)
   _____(positive practice)
4. Jamie doesn't do his homework.
   _____(restitutional correction)
   _____(positive practice)
5. Jamie lies to his parents about bad test grades.
   _____(restitutional correction)
   _____(positive practice)

a. Jamie must apologize for the trouble he has caused and must buy a new toy, worth more than the first, out of his allowance.
b. Jamie must do ten minutes of extra chores for every chore he neglects.
c. Jamie must write an apology to every student and deliver it in person.
d. Jamie must tell the correct story to the people he has lied to and explain his reasons for lying to two additional people.
e. Jamie is taught how to make five toys to be used as presents for other children.
f. Jamie has to make up all his schoolwork on a Saturday, plus one extra hour of work.
g. Jamie is taught quiet, cooperative games to play with other children.
h. Jamie is taught how to score his own tests in the presence of his parents. He puts his own grade on the paper and his parents help him with his mistakes.
i. Jamie is taught how to make a schedule to keep track of his chores (see THE SECRET SPY GAME in Chapter 5).
j. Jamie is taught good study habits and given an incentive for doing his homework everyday (see Chapter 3).

What you should learn from this game is:

Habit #5: Use punishments to instruct the child on how to behave correctly rather than to embarrass or humiliate him.

picture, perfect, positive behavior

The last game in this chapter is the simplest, but it is also the most important. I want you to practice giving praise and affection to the child who has problems in self-control for everything he does that is positive. If you are like many adults who are around this type of child a lot, you may now be thinking, "Like what, for instance?" That question is part of the problem. When children are active and impulsive and get into constant mischief, we are so busy trying to keep up with them that we rarely spend enough time focusing on the things they do right. Their good behavior fades into the background until it is virtually ignored. Like the negative a photographer uses to develop a print, everything is in reverse.

It is not a coincidence that you may be doing this with your own habits as well. Because self-control is such a highly touted value in our culture, and yet at the same time we have an overabundance of temptations, many adults constantly berate themselves for smoking, overeating, nail-biting, and other habits. But how many of us find time to praise ourselves for our positive actions—the hundreds of times that we show self-control by being good to ourselves and others?

However this situation can be changed. The first thing you must do is to ignore as many of the child's annoying behaviors as you can, and concentrate on what he does right. The second thing is to give him praise and affection for even his smallest accomplishment. In psychological terms, this is called *positive reinforcement,* and the principle is that behavior which is reinforced, or rewarded, will occur more often, and behavior which is ignored will tend to fade away. Thus through positive reinforcement we can begin to reverse the negative image we have of the child with problems in self-control, and we will be reversing the image he has of himself as well.

Exactly the same procedure can work with your own bad habits. Praising and rewarding yourself for the good things that you do will focus your attention away from your bad habits, will make you feel better about yourself, and will motivate you to change in whatever direction you desire. Focusing on your "good" behaviors will give you the self-confidence to gain more self-control.

But let's look at an example of how this works with a child and where some of the pitfalls are. Let's take the case of a child, Mike, who is always late for dinner. Let's assume that this is an annoyance to you, but it is far from being the most important problem (you will remember from the first game in this chapter, TARGETS, that you have to keep the heavy artillery, such as the overcorrection procedure, for the most important problems). On Monday the child comes to the dinner table ten minutes late. You should say nothing. On Tuesday, however, he is nine minutes late. Praise him for this! It is not a great improvement, but it is a step in the right direction. You don't have to fall all over yourself, but simply say, "Mike, you got to dinner earlier tonight. That's very good." On Wednesday night, Mike comes to the table 15 minutes late. You ignore this, but you also make no special allowances for him. If he has missed part of the meal, don't go to any special trouble; he can get what he missed later. To go to special trouble would be reinforcing his coming late. (You also might think about what you usually serve at the beginning of the meal. If you serve his favorite foods first, he will be more motivated to come on time.)

On Tuesday Mike comes right on time. This is quite an improvement—the first time he has done it without a hassle for months. So you show your pleasure with a smile, praise, a gesture, or a pat.

Friday comes and Mike is six minutes late for dinner. This deserves praise, even though it is not as good as the night before, but it is still a vast improvement over his usual 15-minute tardiness.

Be careful, however, not to give praise with one hand and take it away with another. One mother told me that she praises her daughter every time she cleans up her room. But when I asked the daughter to imitate her mother giving praise, she said in a sarcastic voice, "Well, I see you *finally* cleaned your room today. That's good. It's about time." Sarcasm is one of a child's worst enemies.

Reinforce any positive steps that the child makes, and don't get discouraged and fall back into old disciplining habits. I can't emphasize enough how powerful this technique can be if it's done correctly. Many children with problems have been helped when the adults in their life used only this one principle of disciplining. But doing it right takes some practice, so here is the game that I want you to play.

Take seven sheets of paper and write one day of the week on the top of each one. Divide each paper in half by drawing a line down the middle. Now I want you to give four instances of encouragement to the child each day (praise, gestures, affection) for anything positive he does and give yourself three "pats on the back" each day for the things you do right. Write what you do to encourage the child on the left-hand side of the page and what you do to encourage yourself on the right-hand side. Carry the paper around with you so that you can write these things down as soon as they occur.

At the end of the week, look at what you wrote on each of the seven pages. If you are like most adults, you will probably find that you did better at the beginning of the week than at the end. By the third or fourth day, some people forget to do it all together. This is because it conflicts with their old habits. So try a little harder each day. Give yourself one-quarter point for each instance of encouraging the child on days one and two, one-half point for each instance of encouragement on days three, four, and five, and one point for each instance of encouragement on days six and seven.

Keep working on:

Habit #6: Give positive reinforcement—praise, affection, gestures, treats—for everything that the child does which is a step toward improving his behavior. Ignore petty annoyances as much as possible.

SCORING THE ADULT GAMES

Here is a review of the scoring for each of the six games that you played in this chapter:

TARGETS: Five points for each behavior that, after a discussion with another adult who knows the child, remained unchanged on target B. Limit 25 points.

CLUES AND CUES: One point for each cue that you identified as part of the child's behavior pattern. Limit 10 points.

RELAX ABOUT THINGS: Two points for each time you practice relaxing. Limit 20 points.

MIRROR, MIRROR ON THE WALL: One point for every time you practice reflecting the child's problem calmly and impartially. Limit 25 points.

LET THE PUNISHMENT OVER-FIT THE CRIME: Two points for each correct answer on the matching game. Limit 20 points.

PICTURE, PERFECT, POSITIVE BEHAVIOR: One-quarter point for each instance of encouragement on days one and two, one-half point for each instance of encouragement on days three, four and five, and one point for each instance of encouragement on days six and seven. Limit 40 points.

Total Possible Points: 140

A Review of the New Disciplining Habits

Even if you forget some of the points of the games in this chapter, try and remember and practice the six new disciplining habits:

1. *Don't think of your child as all bad. Realize that some of his problems are more serious to his growth than others, and put your time and energy into helping him with these problems first.*

2. *Look for cues that tell you that a child is about to misbehave. Try to catch the problem before it starts.*

3. *Relax until you are calm before you discipline a child. You will not be able to help him learn self-control if you can't control your own feelings first.*

4. *Don't criticize when you punish, but rather reflect to the child what has happened by describing and clarifying to him what he has done and what he is feeling.*

5. *Use punishments to instruct the child on how to behave correctly, rather than to embarrass or humiliate him.*

6. *Give positive reinforcement—praise, affection, gestures, treats—for everything the child does which is a step towards improving his behavior. Ignore petty annoyances as much as possible.*

3 How to use this book

The developmental approach used in this book is based on two assumptions: (1) that children with problems in self-control have not learned age-specific skills which we take for granted in other children, and (2) that just as a child can learn to hit a baseball through instruction and practice, so can he learn a new set of skills to help him control his behavior. However, we must also realize that children start with different levels of ability. While nearly every child can hit a baseball, not every child will hit a home run every time at bat. Some children will do better at bunting than slugging. Others will be able to hit one kind of pitch and not another. Still others must be advised that the pitcher is throwing the ball wildly and to wait for a walk. It is the same in learning the skills necessary for self-control. Some children will have more natural ability to learn new skills than others. We must look at each one's progress according to where he started from and what his natural limits are. For some children, the skills you can teach them from this book may open up a whole new way of relating to the world; such a child is like a ball player who makes a slight correction in his swing to connect with the ball. But more often the skills you can teach the child will be used to help him compensate for one problem or another. He may not hit home runs, but he can learn to play the game.

Your role, whether you are the child's parent, teacher, counselor,

31

or other interested adult, is to play games with the child; as you play, you will be instructing the child in new ways to control himself.

The successful teaching of new cognitive, emotional, and behavioral skills will depend on four interrelated factors: 1) the games themselves, (2) the way you relate to the child when you play the games, (3) motivating the child, and (4) documenting the child's progress. The key to being effective lies in the interaction of all four factors, so read through this chapter carefully before proceeding.

THE GAMES

The games in this book are grouped into six areas (Chapters 4 through 9) that form a continuum of sequentially ordered developmental skills. The games within each chapter are also presented in a developmental order, so that the typical child without problems in self-control would be expected to develop the skills focused on in each game in the order that they are presented in the book. While, in general, you will find that the activities in the beginning of the book are more appropriate to children with severe problems and the activities towards the end of the book are more relevant to children with milder problems in self-control, this should not be the only criterion for selecting an activity. The most crucial thing to remember in choosing an activity is that it should be fun for both the child and the adult working with him. In the second place, the activity should address the skill area in which you feel your child's development is lacking.

This is very difficult to assess, even for a professional, and in my own practice I have found that trial and error can be just as effective in choosing the right game as sophisticated diagnostic testing. In any event, those teachers, counselors, or other professionals who may wish to choose games by behavioral objectives should consult the chart in Appendix A.

Finally, you must consider the practical aspects of the activity: Can you spend the time with the child that the activity requires? Do you have a good place to work? Do you have the necessary resources on hand?

The selection of the first games is an important step, and I suggest that you read through the book in its entirety before you make your decision. Remember that since the games form a continuum, you should go backward in the book if the game is too difficult or frustrating for the child, and forward if the game is easily accomplished and not challenging. Note that some games, such as the ones in Chapter 8, are interrelated and the games only can be played in sequence beginning with the first one in the chapter.

How to Relate While You
Play the Games

The relationship that the adult and child will establish is as important as the game you select. The following principles must be followed at all times in working with the impulsive child. Write them on a 3 X 5 card, and take this card with you whenever you work together. Read them *before and after* each activity, and try to correct the mistakes you make (don't worry, you *will* make mistakes, but the trick is to learn from them).

★ Principle 1. *Be Persistent*: Every effort must be made to complete a game. The message to the child must be: I will not let this go wrong; I will not let you fail again. If you find that it is difficult to complete games with the child, make them simpler so that they require less time.

★ Principle 2. *Try to Guarantee Success*: Always guide the child towards choices which will offer him or her success and rewards. Left to his own devices, the impulsive child with a poor self-concept will make choices that reaffirm his low self-esteem.

★ Principle 3. *Set Limits Clearly*: Make it very clear what is acceptable and what is not acceptable when you work together. While you must be able to tolerate the child's typically high activity level, you must not tolerate random destructiveness or aggressiveness. End the game rather than continue in frustration.

★ Principle 4. *Always Show Respect*: Respect everything a child is, and everything he does, and demonstrate this with your actions. Ignore the child when he devalues himself (but don't contradict him), and show him how you express pride in *your* accomplishments.

★ Principle 5. *Define Your Relationship as Positive*: Show the child through your actions and verbal statements that you value your time together. If you cannot do this with complete sincerity, then perhaps you are not the right person to be working with the child.

★ Principle 6. *Help Positive Decision Making*: Give the child choices that are clear and positive. Appropriate decision making is a skill that can be learned, so provide plenty of practice.

★ Principle 7. *Do Not Reinforce Maladaptive Behaviors*: Ignore inappropriate behaviors that the child is using just to get your attention.

★ Principle 8. *Give Social Reinforcement Often While You Play*: Reinforce your child every time he works for a long period of time, shows his motivation to learn, or succeeds at any task. You can do this naturally by giving him praise and affection, by your gestures, and by your body position.

33

⋆ Principle 9. *Guide the Child toward Substituting New Behaviors for Old Ones*: As you work together on various activities and games, your child should be acquiring new skills. Help him use these as a substitute for behaviors that previously got him into trouble. For example, a child who greeted his classmates by pinching them as he went down the hall was taught to shake hands as a greeting instead.

MOTIVATING THE CHILD TO
PLAY THE GAME

The games in this book should be inherently motivating for both the children and adults who play them, because they are fun. But children with problems in self-control are not known for their eagerness to cooperate. To return to the baseball analogy mentioned at the beginning of the chapter, many children love to play that game and do so at any opportunity they get, but the child with poor skills is not likely to be motivated to play because he is used to being embarrassed by his inadequacies and feels frustrated when he fails. The same holds true for children who lack skills in self-control. They have a poor sense of self-esteem, are afraid of failure, and will predictably resist your attempts to teach them games that focus on their problems.

To get past this initial resistance, I recommend using a *token economy reward system*. A token economy system is a popular behavior management technique that motivates the child by giving him a specified number of chips, points, stars, or other "tokens" every time he does a task that would normally be difficult for him. The child can then cash in these tokens for some reward which he highly values. The basic concept should be familiar. It is what most adults do every day: work at difficult tasks for money (a type of token) in order to buy the things they want.

To set up a token economy system with the child you are working with, begin by making a reward list of five to ten things that the child would like to work for. These might be things such as toys, sports equipment, clothes, or activities such as going to a movie or out to dinner with a special person. Then assign a token value to each of the things that the child might want. I use the formula that 25 points equal $1.00, so that if a child I'm working with wants to earn a $10 calculator, he must earn 250 points, but if he wants to earn a comic book, he needs only 13 points. When making up the list of things that the child can earn, I encourage him to put down some things that can be earned for a relatively few tokens, as well as things that he will have to work for over several months. While it is nice to have a child who can save points for something that he really

wants (and that you may want him to have) still it must be completely up
to the child to spend the tokens as he likes. Most children with problems in
self-control will not be savers but will want to spend the tokens as soon as
they are earned. Make sure you live up to your part of the bargain by
always having what the child wants nearby when he is ready to spend his
tokens. Making him wait for something that he has worked hard to earn
can cause a serious breach of trust.

Before you play each game, you must decide how the child will be
earning points, and how many points he will be able to earn each session.
Optimally, I like to give the child a chance to earn from 25 to 50 points
when he is with me and another 25 to 50 points playing the game with
someone else, for example, his parents or teachers. If the child is consistently not earning points, however, then this is a strong indication that
you have chosen games that are too difficult for the child.

DOCUMENTING PROGRESS

In determing whether the child you're working with is really changing,
either through maturation or through your intervention, you must keep
track of the two areas which are most critical to the growth of a child with
problems in self-control.

1. *The child should be able to learn in school at a consistent pace,
despite his impulsivity and activeness.* Many children, particularly below
the ages of eight or nine, can learn in spite of the fact that they never seem
to sit down for a moment and never seem to listen to what you are saying.
Conversely, studies have shown that many hyperactive children who are
put on medication for their impulsivity and distractibility begin to *look* as if
they are learning, for they can now sit quietly in a chair, but in fact, they
do just as poorly in school as when they were very active. To put it simply:
Looks are deceiving. You must keep an accurate record of your child's
school progress by evaluating all his grades and any standardized
achievement tests that he is given. If you feel that your child is not making
consistent progress at any time, you should immediately consult with his
teacher or the learning specialist in your school.

2. *The impulsive child should be able to work independently for
increasing amounts of time.* The second important factor which denotes
progress for the child with poor self-control is that he is able to sit for
longer and longer periods of time working at a task without being
distracted or having to get up from his seat. In order to keep track of the
child's growth in this area, select a school-related task that is interesting
and challenging to the child, but not too difficult. This may be a

35

homework assignment in the area of math, language, social studies, or science. It should not be the child's best or worst subject, but something in between. Explain to the child that you want to help him to learn to concentrate, because it will help him in school and later when he goes to work.

    To make this into more of a game, give the child a "time card" like the one shown in Fig. 3 to mark the time in and out of every work period. You can buy a rubber stamp at an office supply store to mark when the child begins and ends his work. Explain to the child that you want him to work for as long as he can, but when he feels that he just cannot concentrate anymore, he should stop and "punch out." Note that the time card in Fig. 3 has a space for you to comment on the child's study habits. Use this for praise but not for criticism. You must expect that the child will have some days when he just cannot concentrate. Don't you have days like that? It is most important for you and the child to be realistic about his study habits so that you can work together on improving them.

    Keep all the time cards so that you have a record of the child's

Figure 3

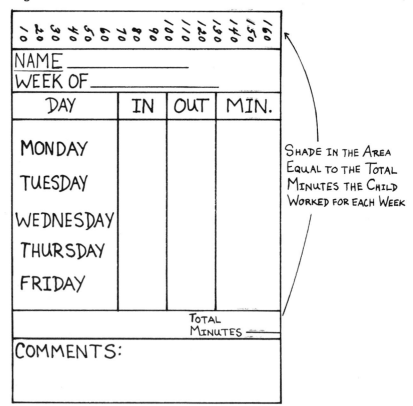

SHADE IN THE AREA EQUAL TO THE TOTAL MINUTES THE CHILD WORKED FOR EACH WEEK

progress from week to week. Placing the cards together, as shown in Fig. 4, will give you a graph of the child's progress, which should show a steady upward slope.

Try to measure the child's attention span at the same time each week. Work along beside him to provide him with a good role model and to help him with problems when they occur. When he has achieved certain goals (for example, doubling, tripling, and quadrupling the time he can work independently), you may wish to give him a special treat. Rejoice in even the smallest progress; remember that this is a very difficult personality trait to change. However, patience and persistence will pay off. When your child has reached this goal, you may wish to involve other family members in this quiet, study period. You will be amazed at how fast good study habits can become contagious when they are reinforced and modeled by parents. Parents who want to watch television while their children work will probably have less success.

Figure 4

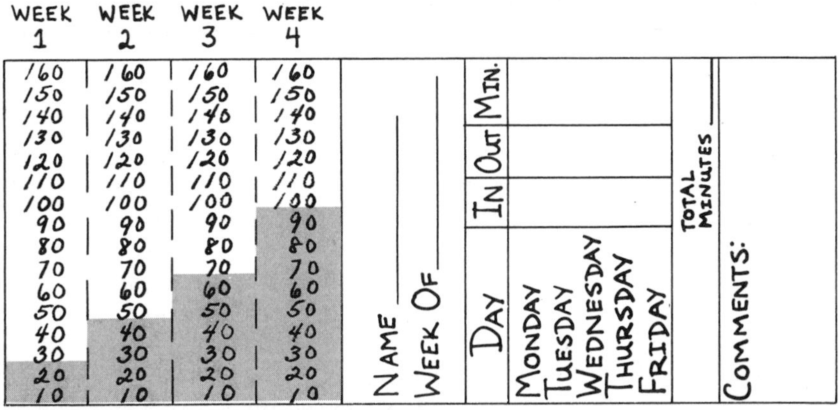

OVER-LAP EACH TIME CARD TO SHOW A BAR GRAPH OF THE TOTAL MINUTES THAT THE CHILD WORKS EACH WK.

37

Teaching the preschool child self-control

Nearly everything a preschool child does is an issue of self-control. With every month, the child develops new control over muscles and movements. Every new word uttered is a portrait in self-control as the child inhibits the instinct to act and thus satisfy immediate needs but chooses instead to communicate. Even new discoveries involve self-control. When given a new toy, the infant tries to eat it or throw it or both, but the older child examines it, manipulates it, uses it as he or she has seen other children do, or invents imaginative games. Children bring their history of past experiences to bear in controlling themselves in each new action.

Parents are acutely aware of each new gain that children make in controlling their bodies and then their emotions and finally their overall behavior. With each new step the child becomes more independent and the parents breathe a sigh of relief. When the child learns to use a spoon and then a fork, this frees the parent's hands to eat his or her own dinner. When the child walks, sore backs are spared. When toilet training is achieved, a messy and time-consuming chore is eliminated. As children develop emotional control, they cry less, wait longer, and tell their folks what is bothering them. So parents have a heavy investment in their children's self-control, and for this reason, the issue of who is going to control whom can be a pervasive one in the preschooler's life.

Problems in self-control usually begin when the child is between two and two and a half years old, which is when toilet training begins. At this time the issue of control focuses on the child's readiness and willingness to perform a task for himself which his parents are more than pleased to relinquish. Recent research by Azrin and Foxx (1978) suggests that the wide variety of experiences that parents have in toilet training reflects more their varying attitudes toward child-rearing than differences in readiness among children. With a group of 200 children between the ages of twenty months and four years, Azrin and Foxx have shown that children can be toilet-trained (perhaps the most emotionally complex issue of self-control) in a matter of hours rather than months. The key to their method of toilet training is the impact of several psychological principles working together. Some people call this the *shotgun approach,* firing off many shots that scatter over a wide area in the hope that at least one will hit the target. I also believe in using several different approaches simultaneously, coming at the problem from different angles and perspectives. And I particularly emphasize this in teaching preschoolers self-control.

Using behavior modification techniques to discipline a child (see Chapter 2) along with the developmental activity approach of this book is an example of a multiple psychological approach. This approach addresses the issue of self-control from two sides: (1) adult expectations for a child to conform become reasonable and consistent and (2) the child develops the inner resources that enable him to meet these expectations.

The activities in this chapter are not designed to address a short-term issue of control, such as toilet training, but rather an entire developmental period, which roughly spans the years from three to eight. This is the period when the child must control himself enough to learn in school. While there are many other factors involved in success in school, studies have shown that children who cannot control themselves are the ones who are most frequently identified as problems by their teachers, and who also are prone to academic failure. Considering that studies have also shown that a child's early school experiences can be highly predictive of his entire school career, the issue of self-control in the preschool and early school-age child becomes even more critical. In this chapter, we will look at the most significant behaviors that the child will need in order to be identified as a good learner in school: the ability to sit for reasonable periods of time and the ability to work independently. Let me emphasize that impulsiveness and high activity levels in a child are not related to intelligence or basic ability to learn, but rather that these factors are associated with early problems in school which may affect even the brightest children.

Like all the games in this book, the games for preschoolers have a dual prupose: to help the child learn self-control and to help the adult working with the child acquire a better understanding of the child's point of view, his strengths, and his weaknesses.

TEACHING A CHILD TO STAY IN HIS SEAT

"He can't sit down for a minute" is a common complaint made by both parents and teachers. However, this is usually an inaccurate statement. There are very few preschool children who literally can't sit down for 10 or 15 minutes at a time, but these may not be the times that the parents want them to sit. Even the most active child will sit still when he is very interested in something. As parents and teachers of active children, you should follow the general steps listed below to set the stage for good work habits.

1. *Frequently provide activities that the child likes.* Try not to overpower the child with your own value system when he chooses activities. If the child likes to mess, give him the opportunity to do this with finger paints, water, or clay in a place you can easily clean. If he likes to run and tumble, make sure that he has an opportunity to do this in a safe environment where he will not have to be too closely supervised. (See the section on playgrounds in Lynda Madarog's book *Child's Play,* listed in the Suggested Reading Section, for ideas on how to make your own inexpensive playground equipment).

2. *Reinforce the child for times when he sits quietly.* Do this with praise ("You're sitting so nicely, just like a big boy!"), through gestures of approval, and by generally giving him attention for these quiet periods. Commonly, adults ignore the child when he is quiet, taking this time to rest themselves, and only give the child attention when he is very active or needs to be supervised. However, according to basic psychological principles this is just the opposite of what you should do. Instead, give him attention when he is quiet and try to let him find his own limits when he is overly active.

3. *Avoid situations that require the child to sit for unrealistic periods of time.* If your child cannot sit at the dinner table for more than five minutes, then it is unrealistic to take him to a restaurant where he must sit for at least 30 minutes. Although this will be inconvenient for you at times, it is in the best interest of the child and your sanity. When you ask a child to do something that he simply can't do yet, you set him up for frustration and failure.

4. *Pay attention to the activity level of the child's home or school room.* It is hard to ask an active child to be still when others around him are up and about, when loud, fast-beat music is playing, or when there is simply a tremendous amount of stimulation.

Here are some activities that will reinforce the child's interest in sitting.

40

the magic seat

Have you ever seen a MAGIC SEAT? When you sit on it, strange things happen. Music plays, the TV goes on, toys start to work. The trick is simple: place a spring release switch (available at most electrical supply stores) under a light pillow which is secured firmly to the seat of a child-size chair. The switch should be spliced to an extension cord, into which electrical gadgets can then be plugged (see Fig. 5). The weight of the child sitting down on the pillow triggers the switch, and turns on any type of electrical gadget. When the child gets off his chair, the gadget goes off too. The principle is as simple as the apparatus. When a behavior (sitting) is followed by a highly desired event (music or TV watching, for example), the first behavior will increase dramatically.

Set up a seat like the one shown in Fig. 5. At first the child will be fascinated by the concept of the switch and will probably jump on and off the chair. The idea is that he will want the gadget turned on to stimulate him so that eventually he will want to sit for longer and longer periods of time to get the reward. You can build up the child's tolerance for sitting—

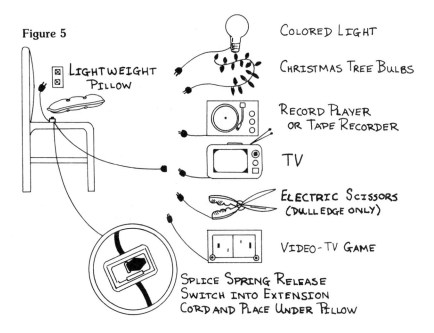

Figure 5

LIGHTWEIGHT PILLOW

COLORED LIGHT

CHRISTMAS TREE BULBS

RECORD PLAYER OR TAPE RECORDER

TV

ELECTRIC SCISSORS (DULL EDGE ONLY)

VIDEO-TV GAME

SPLICE SPRING RELEASE SWITCH INTO EXTENSION CORD AND PLACE UNDER PILLOW

CAUTION: NEVER LEAVE A CHILD UNSUPERVISED AROUND ELECTRICAL APPARATUS

41

and keep his interest—by changing the gadget which the switch controls so as to go from a momentary reward to a reward that takes longer and longer periods of sitting to appreciate. Here is an example of what I mean:

1. Colored light bulb. The child will be fascinated just turning it on.
2. String of colored Christmas light bulbs. The child will want to see the pattern of light that the bulbs make.
3. Tape recorder or record player with the child's favorite song. The child will want to sit long enough to hear the whole song.
4. The TV. The child must sit for 15 to 30 minutes to watch his favorite cartoon or TV show.
5. Electric scissors. These can be obtained at most toy stores for about $5. They are not sharp, but when plugged in will vibrate in such a way that they can cut paper. Other electric toys can also be used in the same way and may stimulate the child for indefinite periods of time, particularly if you play with him.
6. Video TV games. Although these involve some initial cost (from thirty to several hundred dollars), they can be very effective in improving the attention span of an active child. Target games, with an adjustable speed mechanism, are good for learning hand-eye motor coordination and can be played by one child.

CAUTION: *These activities must be supervised at all times by an adult. Most active children will want to explore and play with the electrical apparatus, and this is potentially dangerous.*

the best seat in the house

It should go without saying that a child with problems in staying seated should have a comfortable place to sit, but sometimes this simple fact is overlooked. Make sure the child's chair is his size. His feet should be able to rest flat on the floor. The back of the chair should give him good support but should not be too hard.

But chairs can be more than just posturally correct, they can be special too. Don't you have a special chair in the house? One whose color, fabric, position, or design seems to fit you just right? Grown-ups get emotionally attached to their furniture. For whatever reason, many people have a favorite chair which is theirs alone and which has a special meaning to them beyond its comfort.

This activity is designed to have the child who doesn't like to sit learn to enjoy the feeling of having a special place to sit, to relax, and to work.

There are many ways to make the child's seat the best one in the house. Remodeling can range from simple decals, to soft cushions, to a special paint job, to making his own chair. Bruce Palmer's book, listed in the Suggested Reading section, tells how to make a barrel chair, a slot chair, a lounge chair, and even a wing chair, all out of corrugated cardboard (see Fig. 6). The idea is to capture the child's interest and imagination. Be as elaborate as you like as long as the chair remains comfortable and doesn't itself become a distraction to the child.

a sticky chair

Did you ever feel like taping a child to a chair? I'll bet you did. Did you ever ask a child to pretend he was taped to a chair? Try it. Say, "I want you to make believe that there is sticky tape on the chair, and see if you can convince me that you really are stuck to the chair." Show him how to do it. Use *mime*. If you are a good mime, you pretend that you are unrolling the tape and placing it all over the seat. You sit and then try to

Figure 6

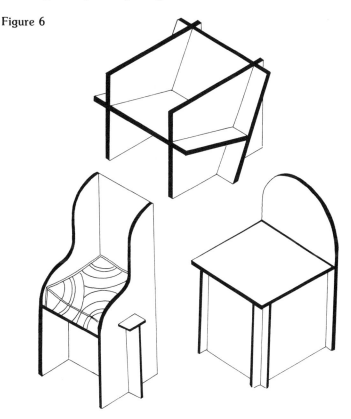

get up, but you can't do it. You show surprise and amazement on your face. You push against the arms, but you can't budge. You pit one set of muscles against the other. Your abdomen presses down while your buttocks press up. It's fun if you can get into it.

Actors sometimes use games like this to physically understand and express the emotions involved in a particular event. Similarly, this theatrical game can be used to make the child aware of the muscles and body energy involved in sitting. Exaggerating the action of sitting heightens the awareness of the body. Not all children will understand the concept, but it's a fun game, and good for you to try too. Understanding the active child also means completely understanding what you are expecting from him: you want him to use a complex system of muscle control and relaxation to enable him to resist his urge to get up and move.

If the child likes this game, practice it often. It's a good isometric exercise. Sometimes you can get him to sit a few more minutes at dinner or when drawing if you remind him that he should "tape himself to his chair."

INCREASING THE PRESCHOOLER'S ATTENTION SPAN

the activity menu

If you are really serious about increasing the preschool child's attention span, you must take a very systematic and analytic approach. Begin by watching your child. Watch your child for not less than three hours, spread over three typical days. Watch him when he is alone at various activities throughout the day and time him with a stopwatch during each activity. The activity can be anything at all—eating a cracker, putting together a puzzle, spilling water in the bath, even daydreaming. Only two things are necessary: he must be doing the activity himself, and he must be reasonably persistent in staying with the activity (for example, repeating the acting several times rather than doing it only once and moving to something else).

Record the activities on the Activity Menu shown in Fig. 7. If you have fewer than five activities, you should observe more activities. Children have a large repertoire of things that keep them interested, and you will see this if you just watch them carefully. In the "theme" column you should write down the thing or things about the activity that give the child

44

Figure 7 ACTIVITY MENU

Activity	Number of Minutes Spent at Activity	Theme	Preference

pleasure. These might include: emptying and filling, running, spinning, coloring, cutting, messy liquids such as paints, water, music, books, writing, and so forth. Write down the number of minutes the child has spent in each activity and then, in the last column, rank the activities according to the amount of time that the child spends on each. Activities that are most pleasurable will be the ones that the child spends more time doing, and these should be ranked first.

Don't be discouraged if the child only spends a minute or two even at the activities he really likes. Remember, we're just getting started. There are three ways to increase the child's attention span by expanding on his natural interests. First of all, try joining him in his activities—on his terms. Starting with his first preference, sit down with him and participate in the activity by mirroring whatever he is doing. Perform an activity parallel to what he is doing, but of course do it at your own tempo and follow your own interests. The child will be pleased that you have joined him and may or may not want to interact with you. Don't be concerned with this. Rather, try and enjoy the activity yourself and see just why your child likes it.

A second approach is to reinforce the child verbally by showing your interest and approval in his activity. Comment on how well he plays, on how much fun he is having, on how it makes you happy to see him have fun. You may join in his play, but be careful not to change the activity to suit your interests rather than his.

The third approach is to combine two pleasurable activities for the child. One theory about overactive children is that they take in information so quickly that they are forever bored and are always looking for more than one thing to interest them. So try doubling up on the child's interests. If the child likes to roll trucks and listen to music, then have him do these activities at the same time. (There are many records about trucking with truck stories and truck noises.) If the child likes to paint and also to build and knock down blocks, then show him how to stack cardboard blocks. Milk cartons can be made into inexpensive blocks (see Bernie Zubrowski's book, listed in the Suggested Readings, on how to make them) and targets can be painted on them. Use your imagination to pair up interesting activities.

Now take another look at your child. Do another hour or two of observation, and make up a second Activity Menu. Total the number of minutes recorded for his five favorite activities and compare it with the total of the first menu. Is there an increase in the total amount of minutes? There should be. Have the activities changed? How about the themes? What have you learned?

Now for the final and most important step—increasing the child's attention span while he does productive activities. The principle is simple: When you pair a pleasurable activity with a neutral or even an unpleasant

46

TITLE   : Games to grow on : activities to help children learn self control
CALL NUMBER : LB1029.G3S5 nuppr
BARCODE   : 3937100481846
PATRON NAME : Salisbury, Chandra
ADDRESS   :
TELEPHONE   : 208-794-7943
PICKUP AT   : NNU Riley Library

one, the less pleasurable activity should become more tolerable. Choose the productive activities carefully. They should be a help to you, but on the other hand, if the child has shown a strong dislike for the activity in the past, this would not be a good place to start. Here are a few suggestions:

Pleasurable Activity	Productive Activity	Combination
Water play	Cleaning	Have the child help wash the car, outside furniture, bathroom tile.
Moving to music	Sorting chores	Select a song and make up a dance to set the table, pick up toys, hang up clothes.
Running	Errands	Have the child run to your neighbor's to pick something up, or to the mailbox, or to the store.

As you can see, the idea is to channel your child's interests and energies in a positive direction, thus increasing his attention span for productive activities. For the time being, you must forget about efficiency and even the correctness or completeness of the activity. Don't remind your child of the toys he didn't pick up; praise him for the ones he did pick up. If the child becomes more interested in the water than in the car he is helping you wash, remember: You get distracted sometimes too!

INCREASING THE CHILD'S FINGER AND HAND CONTROL

Many children who lack self-control also have problems in controlling their hands and fingers. They do not hold a pencil easily, may have difficulty copying geometric shapes, and may find that a pair of scissors is their worst enemy. This is not usually a serious developmental problem—some children simply mature late in this area—but it can become serious if it contributes to a child's frustrations.

The general rule to follow in helping a child improve his finger and hand control and coordinate his movements is: Practice makes perfect. Unfortunately, this is an axiom that most impulsive children will rebel against since practice means frustration and frustration is just what they cannot tolerate. So to offset the frustration, you must offer high-interest activities, such as the ones listed below.

finger-puppet dances

There are many finger puppets available in toy stores at low cost, or you can make your own (see Fig. 8). Wearing one puppet on the index

47

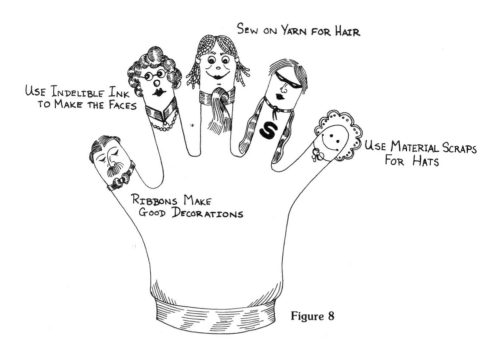

SEW ON YARN FOR HAIR

USE INDELIBLE INK TO MAKE THE FACES

USE MATERIAL SCRAPS FOR HATS

RIBBONS MAKE GOOD DECORATIONS

Figure 8

finger of each hand gives the child the freedom to have the puppets dance to many different kinds of music (jigs, marches, folk dances), the more high-spirited the better. You should have two puppets of your own and should show the child how the puppets can dance in a coordinated rhythmic fashion (as opposed to random flailings, which some children will choose). Moving both hands and arms together helps the child learn to control both sides of his body at the same time, a problem for many learning-disabled youngsters. Next, have the child put one puppet on his index finger and one on his thumb and do a chicken peck dance (to the tune of something like "Turkey in the Straw") in which each puppet pecks forward on alternate sides. This action strengthens the coordination of the thumb and index finger, which are used to hold a pencil as well as to pick up small items.

There are many other kinds of finger games, all of which can be used to strengthen muscles and coordinate movements.

art power

Art has been identified as a way to help children with problems for many years. It is a way for children to express themselves when words are not enough. While art is an excellent free-form expression for children, it

48

is also an excellent way to develop hand-eye coordination. There are thousands of art activities that are fun for children and also help them to develop hand and eye coordination, but for overactive preschool children, I prefer projects that *instruct* the child while he is having fun. This is for two reasons: (1) overactive children have a high incidence of learning problems, so any head start they can get in early school concepts the better; and (2) we must always look at how overactive children learn best. They often do not seem to learn the same way as their calmer peers. So, if an active preschooler learns well through art activities, this could be an important diagnostic factor in his early school career.

For a start, try teaching the child to write his name (or a few other words) using as many different art mediums and parts of the body as you can think of. Have him finger-paint his name (or if this is too hard, just the first letter). Have him do it with each finger of each hand. Use different colors. Have him try it with his big toe (you will probably have to guide his foot yourself).

Roll a ball of clay into a snake and then form it into letters. Cut letters out of paper. Dip string in paint to form his name. Spray-paint the name on a giant poster. Tattoo his name on his arms, legs, and stomach with body makeup (this comes in crayon form). Spell the name with pebbles by gluing them in a box. Use cotton balls to spell his name by gluing them on paper so they look like cartoon smoke signals. Write his name with ketchup on his hamburger and as part of the icing on a cake.

Think of a hundred ways to write his name, and don't forget to ask the child to think of some too. Then have him sit down and do it with a pencil. You've just increased your child's odds of having success by 100 percent. That's ART POWER.

the game of adaptation

So many children have finger and hand movement problems that educators have created a demand for inexpensive adaptive equipment to make writing and other hand-eye coordination activities easier. Here are just a few of the most common ones:

⋆ **Pencil grip:** This is a triangular grip that is slipped onto a regular size pencil. It provides a cushion for the child's fingers and eliminates slipping (about $4 for 25 grips).

⋆ **Letter-tracing stencils:** These allow the child to practice forming perfect letters without having to worry about pencil control (about $4.50).

49

★ **Training scissors:** These scissors have two sets of holes, one outer set for the adult and an inner pair for the child. They come in styles for both right-and left-handed students (about $6).

★ **Large grip scissors:** These scissors have very large polypropylene handles and can be squeezed together to cut by using the hands or arms (about $5).

These items are available from Educational Teaching Aids, 159 Kinzie St., Chicago, Illinois 60610, telephone (312) 644-9438. You may write this company for a catalog or visit a local teachers' supply store, which may carry some of the same items.

But, how do you motivate the child to use these aids? Make it into a game. Reward the child for the improvements he will experience when he uses the adaptive aids. For instance, if you want the child to practice making circles with the pencil grip, say, "How many round cookies can you draw in two minutes? Here is a timer and here is a pencil and we'll see." Let the child do whatever he pleases, then say, "Now this gadget will help you hold the pencil better. It also means you can draw more cookies faster." Put the pencil grip on, set the timer, and say, "Now we'll see how many you can draw in two minutes. And for every additional cookie you draw over what you drew the first time, you'll get a real cookie!"

5 Learning to follow directions

Impulsive children are usually poor listeners. Because they are easily distracted, they may not hear all that you say, or they may not be able to remember what you have said because their minds are racing ahead to something more interesting. My first advice to parents of children who do not listen well is to have their hearing checked. Although physical hearings problems are no more common in impulsive children that in any other children, still we cannot overlook simple and obvious solutions. There are many reasons for hearing loss—from the buildup of ear wax to infections, as well as more severe damage to the delicate mechanisms of the ear. Make sure you have eliminated this possible explanation of your child's poor listening habits by having him tested by a qualified audiologist or speech pathologist. You can get a recommendation for these specialists from your pediatrician.

Having assured yourself that your child hears well, begin with the first three activities that are concerned with the child's ability to understand and process information. Your child's skills at listening will improve with age; however, that may not be of much comfort to you right now. For this reason, the rest of the activities in this chapter are designed to help you find other ways to communicate with your child so that he can learn to follow directions. If the child is not motivated to play one or more of the games, remember that learning new skills and changing old habits is difficult. Refer to the discussion in Chapter 3 on how to motivate a child to play by using tangible rewards.

basic concepts baseball

Miss Swann, a first-grade teacher, told Sam to get in line behind Jill, but he didn't do it. He got in front of Jill instead. Miss Swann didn't think too much of the incident, but later that day she sent Sam down the hall and told him to be back in five minutes. When Sam came back twenty minutes later, she thought, "This is a stubborn boy" and decided to punish him with an extra class assignment. That same afternoon, Sam's teacher graded the class spelling tests, and pulled Sam's paper out of the pile. His name was at the bottom of the page, not in the top right-hand corner as she had directed. The words were all spelled right, but they were arranged haphazardly on the page, and were not numbered the way the teacher had asked. Sam's teacher thought, "This boy won't follow directions—he's a stubborn kid."

Miss Swann was partly right. Sam couldn't follow directions—but not because he was stubborn or disobedient. Sam wanted to follow the directions like the other children, but he misinterpreted the basic concepts in Miss Swann's directions: *behind, five minutes, top right-hand corner, number sequentially, on the left.*

Similar incidents happen daily in every school, but we often fail to recognize the problem. Some children in every grade (particularly in kindergarten through second grade) do not understand basic spatial and time concepts. Usually they get along by looking around at what everyone else is doing, but for some children this doesn't work. Because they don't understand why they are confused and no one else is, they draw attention away from their confusion by acting up, and then they are well on their way to becoming behavior problems—children without self-control.

Knowing fewer concepts than other children in the class is not in itself serious, but it can lead to problems. If left alone, almost all children will eventually learn the basic concepts through trial and error and maturation. Unfortunately, we cannot leave children to develop in a vacuum at their own rate. By far the major part of the teaching done in school takes place in a group situation. A teacher of 20 or 30 children naturally realizes that some children will learn faster and others more slowly, but takes it for granted that all the children in the class will start with all the minimal skills—even though this is often not the case. To make things even more complicated, children, like adults, will try to compensate for their weaknesses and try to hide them.

52

The child who does not know basic space and time concepts does not yet have a serious problem but could develop problems. If adults see a child as disobedient, stubborn, uncooperative (as Miss Swann began to see Sam), it will not be long before the child thinks of himself that way, and begins to act accordingly. To avoid this cycle of defeat, it is important to discover whether a child who does not follow directions does not understand the basic concepts behind them. Playing a game of BASIC CONCEPTS BASEBALL should tell you immediately whether this is a problem with the child that you are working with.

Although I recommend that the game be played with an adult, so that the learning aspects of the game can be emphasized, it can also be

Figure 9

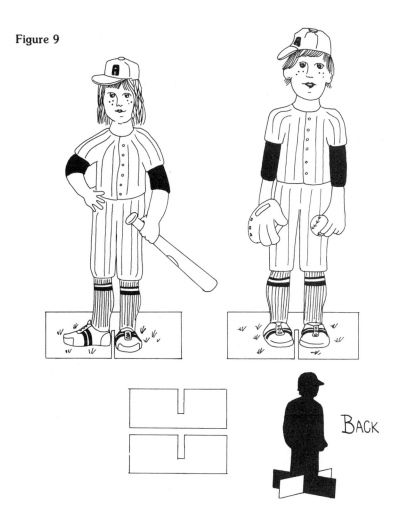

BACK

53

played with other children who have the same abilities. It is designed to be self-correcting, so the child can practice learning concepts by himself. Here are the steps to follow:

1. To construct the game, cut out and assemble the baseball players from Fig. 9 and assemble the baseball field by pasting Figs. 10 and 11

Figure 10

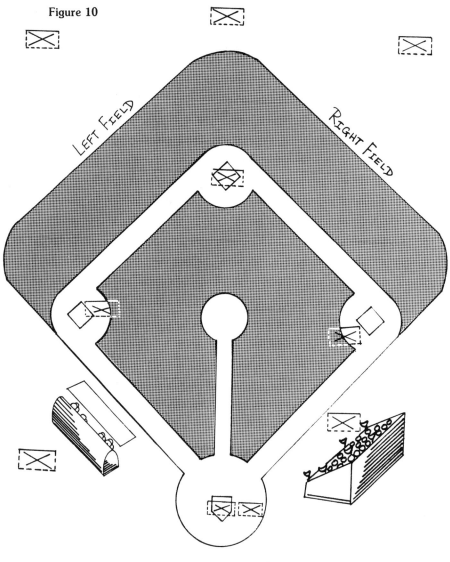

NOTE: CUT ALONG 3 SIDES OF EACH WINDOW

together. You will also need a pair of dice, which can be obtained at most
novelty or drug stores.

2. You will be teaching the child the following concepts, which correspond to the numbers on the dice and appear in the windows of the
playing field:

Figure 11

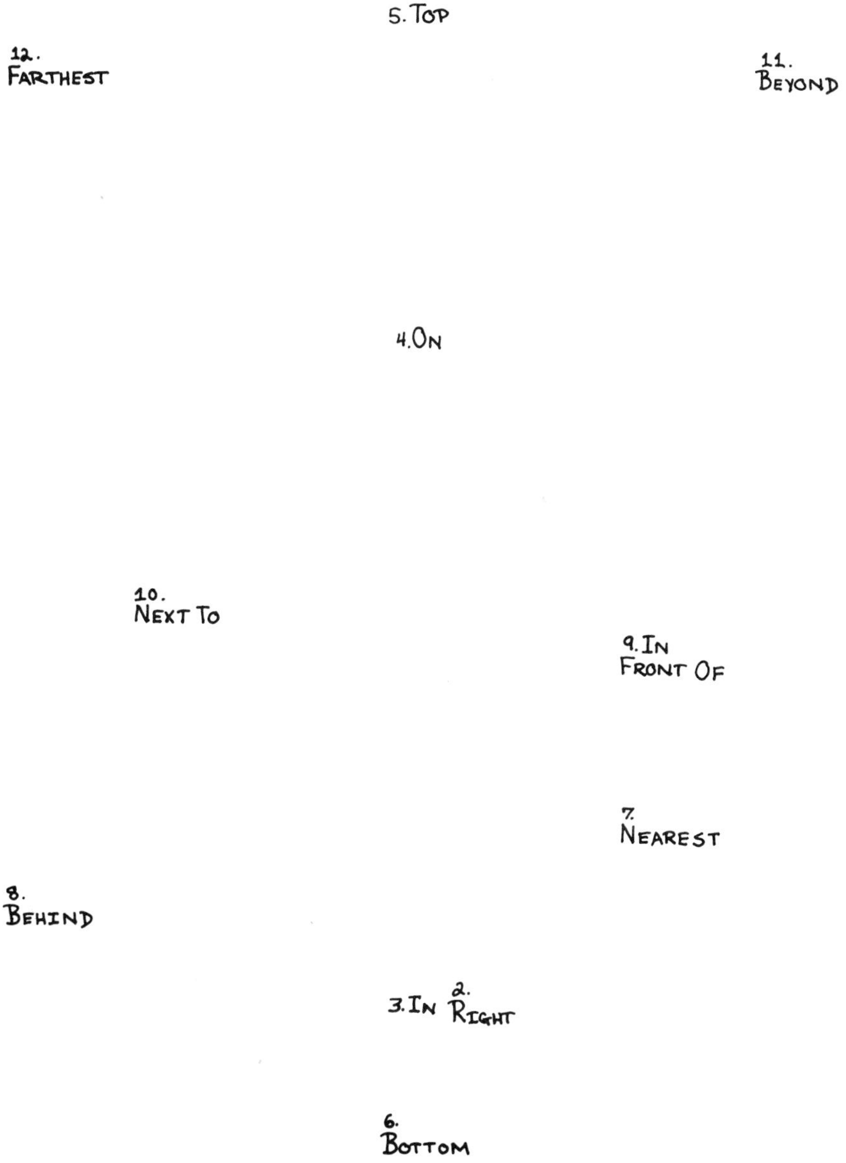

5. TOP

12.
FARTHEST

11.
BEYOND

4. ON

10.
NEXT TO

9. IN
FRONT OF

7.
NEAREST

8.
BEHIND

3. IN RIGHT

6.
BOTTOM

1. There is no 1 since you are using two dice
2. right
3. in
4. on
5. top
6. bottom
7. nearest
8. behind
9. in front of
10. next to
11. beyond
12. farthest

3. To play, the child must roll the dice so that a number between 2 and 12 comes up. Read the child the direction below that corresponds to the number on the dice:

2. Put the player *to the right* of the batter's box.
3. Put the player *in* the batter's box.
4. Put the player *on* second base.
5. Put the player at the *top* of the playing board.
6. Put the player at the *bottom* of the playing board.
7. Put the player on the X *nearest* to the bleachers.
8. Put the player *behind* the dugout.
9. Put the player *in front of* first base.
10. Put the player *next to* third base.
11. Put the player on the X *beyond* right field.
12. Put the player on the X *farthest* from the bleachers.

4. The child must then put the baseball player on the X that corresponds to the spatial concept in the directions. To see if he is right, he must lift the window the X is on and there he should see the correct written concept and the number that corresponds to the number on the dice. Each time the child gets a right answer, he should mark the score sheet (Fig. 12). If he rolls the number of a direction he has already gotten correct, he should roll the dice again. The child wins when all the directions on the score sheet have been marked off in one session.

5. If the child gets a wrong answer, he simply takes another turn.

6. The adult does not take a turn at this game, but rather supervises the child's play by reading him the directions and helping him with difficult concepts. The adult may wish to give the child a special prize or other reward when he has learned all the concepts.

7. There are many adaptations of this game—here are just a few:

For groups of two to four children, make one copy of the

Figure 12   SCORECARD FOR BASIC CONCEPTS BASEBALL

Number	Concept	*Check here when child demonstrates understanding*
2	right	————
3	in	————
4	on	————
5	top	————
6	bottom	————
7	nearest	————
8	behind	————
9	in front of	————
10	next to	————
11	beyond	————
12	farthest	————

score sheet for each child and have the children take turns rolling the dice. The first child to fill in his score sheet wins. This is an excellent way to teach children, because they learn from their friends, but you must be careful to choose children of about the same ability so the child you are working with has an equal chance to win.

You may teach other concepts by constructing similar games from larger magazine pictures (such as the ones found in *Life*) and using small dolls or toy animals as players. Cut out windows in the picture and construct a game board like the baseball field, which shows numbers and the concepts in windows cut out from the pictures.

In choosing new concepts to learn, you will probably want to choose some easy ones and some that are more difficult. Number the more difficult ones 6, 7, and 8, for these will be the numbers that will

57

come up most often on the dice, and the child will have the most practice in learning them.

When the child has learned the spatial concepts in this game, you must make sure that he can use these same concepts in real-life situations. The simplest way to make sure the child can generalize these concepts is to give him directions using the same concepts you have been working on while taking out and putting away the game. For instance, you can say, "Put the game board *on* the table *by* the window" or "Please get me the dice—they're in the box *farthest* away from me." Let the other adults who interact with the child know about the concepts he is learning, and have them give him similar practice. Make sure to give the child a lot of praise as he masters each concept.

someone says

Simon Says is a popular game with children and one which helps them learn to control their movements by listening intently. It is an excellent exercise in learning control for the impulsive child when played in small groups or even alone. The variation, renamed SOMEONE SAYS, is designed to keep the child's interest while he practices very specific, directed movements.

Explain to the child that if he can play for five minutes without getting caught, he will win a prize or a token to purchase a prize (see the section on motivating children to play games in Chapter 3.) Focus the game around a theme which encompasses a positive series of activities with directions such as "SOMEONE SAYS put away your toys" or "SOMEONE SAYS make the bed." It is our hope that the "someone" will eventually be the child himself, who will get pleasure out of doing purposeful and productive activities and will understand that he can get praise for these activities anytime he wants.

You must rig the first game so that the child will win and in the process complete the activities you want him to do. If the child has a very short attention span, then you must make the game very, very short and require only a few purposeful movements. Eventually, the child will build up to paying more attention and performing more complex activites. Here is an example of a game played with a boy who had an attention span of less than two minutes. I have added my own comments, along with what I actually said to the boy, to help you get a feel for how to help such a child succeed.

The Place: The boy's classroom
The Time: Ten minutes before lunch
Name of Game: SOMEONE SAYS GET READY FOR LUNCH

I Said	Comments
"SOMEONE SAYS put your paper away."	Joe slowly put the few pieces of paper on his desk in the inside compartment.
"SOMEONE SAYS straighten your chair."	Joe did this.
"SOMEONE SAYS go sharpen your pencil and put it in your desk."	Joe ran to the sharpener, sharpened the pencil quickly, and ran back to his seat. He did not put the pencil in the desk, so I pantomimed to him the second part of the command. He then did it.
"Put your pencil in your shoe." (Note: Someone did not say to do this, so he should not perform the action.)	Even though Joe knew how to play the game, as I watched him he seemed frozen, wrestling with the decision as to whether to do this foolish act. When I gave him a cue by rolling my eyes, he relaxed and waited for the next command.
"Look at the back of your neck." (Note: again Joe should not do this.)	This was so silly that Joe immediately saw it as a false direction. He relaxed.
"Now SOMEONE SAYS sit with your hand on your desk and wait for the lunch bell."	To help Joe change his thought processes back into following directions, I emphasized the word "Someone." I timed the game so that he only had to sit about one minute before the bell rang.
"That's terrific, Joe! You didn't make even one mistake, so you get the 5 points (25 points bought him a small toy). I'm very proud of you and tomorrow we'll try it again."	You'll note that in playing this game, SOMEONE SAYS only things that are appropriate to the activity. When I didn't want him to follow my direction I gave a silly command. However, I would never give a command that demanded an inappropriate behavior, for this might be too much of a temptation.

You can help your child learn to listen and think about what he hears by giving him cues (nods, winks, pantomime), by emphasizing certain words, and by making it very clear what you *really* expect him to do (in this case, get ready for lunch). With Joe, I played this game for ten consecutive days. Each time I made the game just a little different. By the eleventh day, Joe had won two small toys, and these were given to him just before the lunch bell rang. On that day, before I came in, he had cleared his desk, sharpened his pencil, and was sitting quietly. He did this the same way every day for the rest of the school year.

NEW WAYS TO FOLLOW DIRECTIONS

There are other ways to give children directions than just talking to them. If children have trouble understanding what is said to them, we can communicate visually as an *adjunct* to our oral directions. Usually children will favor either an auditory (hearing) type of communication or a visual one, and when a child has a learning or behavioral problem, you should focus on whatever works, whatever his strength is. The following games will help the child learn to follow directions even if he has trouble paying attention to or understanding what you say.

say it with signs

In the past five years, special educators have found that sign language has value as a communication tool, not only for the deaf but for the child with perfectly normal hearing. Children like to use gestures because they are like a secret code. For children who are visually-oriented rather than hearing-oriented, sign language can be a clear, simple message when everything else is a lot of mixed-up noise. There are advantages for the adult too. I remember several months of trying to teach my one-year-old to say "please" when she wanted food. For some reason she wouldn't catch on. So I was constantly reminding her: "What do you say when you want something? Say 'please' first. Remember the magic word?" I was getting frustrated with her inability to learn and this came out in the tone of my voice, which naturally worked against the whole purpose of my course in manners. Then one day I held up my index finger at the same time that I asked for a "please." I did it again at her next meal. Then I held up my finger for a third time, but I said nothing, and she said "please." I communicated through a gesture, through sign language. From then on I never had to ask her to say "please" again. She actually didn't say "please" automatically, but now I had only to hold up my index finger to get the response I thought was important for her to learn. It saved my voice a lot of wear and tear, and it saved me the frustration of repeating myself and twenty times a day. Even more, it was a game that my daughter and I both enjoyed, and teaching her manners suddenly became fun.

Here are ten signs that can be used with an impulsive or overactive child.

You will probably want to teach these signs in two groups, waiting until the child has mastered the first group before going on to the second one. Most children will learn the signs quickly in 15 to 20 minutes. They will need practice however, and that is where the game comes in.

Make believe that you and the child are two astronauts setting up a camp on the moon and that your voice projectors have gone dead. You are the captain and the child is the first mate, and you want him to make a snack for both of you before you go out and scout the terrain. Then you must stop talking. Using the ten signs you have learned, as well as any

Figure 13

COME: With Your Index Fingers Out, Roll Your Hands Towards Your Body

QUIET: Begin with Your Finger on Your Lips, Then Move Both Hands Down and Out from Your Mouth

GOOD: Place the Tips of Your Fingers on Your Chin and Move Your Hand Out

LOOK: Point to Your Eyes, Then Twist Your Hand and Point Out

SIT: Bring the Right, Middle, and Index Fingers Down to the Same Fingers of the Left Hand

YES: Move Your Fist Up and Down in Front of You

TRY: Shape Both Hands as Shown and Move Them Down and Out From the Chest

PLEASE: Rotate Your Palm in a Circle on Your Chest

NO: Bring Your Index and Middle Finger Together in One Motion To Your Thumb

STOP: Chop Your Right Hand into the Palm of Your Left

61

other gestures you wish, have him make a simple sandwich, set places for you both, and pour each of you a drink. If he tries to talk at some time, remember to remind him that this is against the rules, and you should use the sign for "quiet." When the food is all out, sit down together and eat, and then you may talk. If he has forgotten some of the signs or didn't understand some of your gestures, go over these with him. When you are through, you should reverse roles, the child being the captain and you the first mate. He must now tell you, with sign language and gestures, how to clean up and where to put everything away.

Now that you have a way of communicating nonverbally with the child, you should explain that this will be your own special way of talking to him. When you want something really important, you will say it with signs. I know one teacher who used this game effectively with a very active child in her class. She made allowances for his need to be up and around, but when she needed an absolutely quiet classroom, she gave him signs to "sit" and "be quiet." Because this boy recognized the respect his teacher had for him and liked their secret code, he immediately obeyed without a word being spoken.

Don't forget to reward the child with praise or with some concrete reward when he has learned this new way to communicate.

the secret treasure map game

When I was a child I loved to make maps. I'd bury objects beneath stones and leaves, jot down secret notes and diagrams, and then dig up the buried objects a few days later. My best friend and I would pass maps back and forth in class showing where we would meet after school, where our adventures would take place, and where the enemy lay in wait. Then there were scavenger hunts with clever clues and diagrams and great prizes for the team that could follow the directions the fastest.

Maps miniaturize the world for children; they make life simpler and more concrete. They give children guideposts at their own level, and make following directions a game that energizes the real world with a child's fantasy.

The SECRET TREASURE MAP GAME introduces the child to map reading as a new way of following an adult's directions. The basic rules are simple: the adult hides toys at different places in a room, and the child must find them by following the arrows on the treasure map. Although the game itself is simple, it can be used to teach many complex cognitive skills. These skills include: (1) the ability to translate abstract directions into concrete actions, (2) the ability to follow a sequence of directions, (3) the ability to incorporate directions into problems that must be solved, and

(4) the ability to see directions as a set of interlocking steps. The four variations of the SECRET TREASURE MAP GAME are meant to teach each of these direction-following skills in turn. Each one gets a little more difficult, and not all children will be able to reach the fourth variation. Remember that the primary emphasis of this game is on the child's ability to follow written (visual) communications from an adult.

VARIATIONS OF THE SECRET TREASURE MAP GAME

⋆ **Game 1**—Understanding that maps represent the real world: Draw a map of a room that the child is familiar with, such as the one shown in Fig. 14. Draw in the prominent features of the room, such as furniture, doors, and windows, and explain to the child that this is a "picture" of the room showing where everything in it is located. Go into the room and show him where you and he are located and how everything in the room corresponds to the pictures on the map. Then say, "See these arrows? They show you where small toys are located. See the number 1? That means it is the first place to look. The arrow points behind the chair. Now let's go and see what is there. (Take the child behind the chair and find the

Figure 14   THE SECRET TREASURE MAP

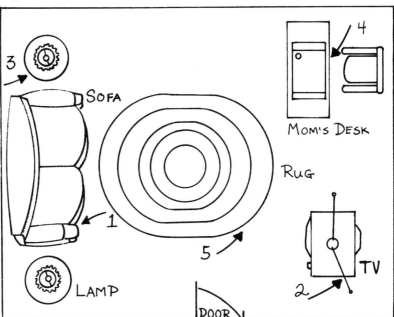

small surprise that you had previously hidden.) Now see if you can find the four other toys. Follow the arrows, and you'll find them." If the child has difficulty, you may wish to give him some hints the first time you play the game, such as saying "warm" when he is close to the prize and "cold" when he is not. The next time you play the game, however, see if you can put your clues on the map. For instance, you can color-code the map by making each arrow a different bright color. Then hide the prizes under large circles the same color as the arrow so that they will stand out more for the child. Try to let the child rely on the map as much as possible. You may even want to leave the room while he is searching and have him come to you when all five prizes are found.

⋆ **Game 2**—<u>Learning to follow a sequence of directions</u>: Using the same type of map as in Game 1, hide five new surprises in different places. Then photocopy four extra maps, number them 1 through 5, and mark where to find *only one prize* on each map. Map 1 should show where to find prize 1, map 2 should show where to find prize 2, and so forth. Now you are going to hide four of the maps so that the child will find a new map each time he finds a prize. Hide map 2 with prize 1, map 3 with prize 2, map 4 with prize 3, and map 5 with prize 4. Give the child map 1 and say "There are five prizes in this room. Each time you find a prize, you will also find a map showing you where the next prize is. You must go in the same order as the numbers or you may not find all the prizes."

⋆ **Game 3**—<u>Using directions in combination with other problems</u>: Hide only one prize in the room, but give the child a map which shows five arrows (as in Fig. 14). Then give him a math problem to do, one that you know he can solve without too much difficulty. The answer to the math problem should be either 1, 2, 3, 4, or 5, and that number will indicate which number arrow points to the prize. He may wish to take a trial-and-error approach and look where each of the five arrows points, but you should encourage him toward the more efficient method of simply solving the problem to show him exactly where the prize is.

⋆ **Game 4**—<u>Seeing directions as a series of interlocking steps</u>: For this game, you must hide a prize in a different room from that in which you hide the clues. The clues must be fitted together in order to tell the child where the prize is hidden. The clues might be different words (for example, *THE PRIZE IS IN THE COOKIE JAR*) or if the child can't read, take a

        1   2   3 4 5   6   7

photograph of the area of the room where the prize is hidden and paste a star or dot exactly where the prize is hidden. Then cut the photograph into four or five pieces like a jigsaw puzzle and put each piece into an envelope. Mark the envelopes with the same numbers as the arrows on the map, and hide them around the room. When the child finds all the

64

clues (either words or parts of a picture), he can put them together to find the treasure.

Since you are trying to build up skills in the child, you should have the child play the same game several times until he can do it with ease. Small toys make good prizes and really motivate the child to try; however, you can also use chips or some other tokens which can be cashed in for something else the child wants (see the section on motivating the child to play games in Chapter 3).

finding the way to work

When the impulsive child has acquired the basic concepts involved in map reading presented in the SECRET TREASURE MAP GAME, he is ready to use maps as a way toward independence. At least one child in every classroom will have difficulty understanding the instructions given by his teacher. This may be because he is distracted in group situations, because he cannot remember a series of statements, or for both reasons. This type of child may literally be "lost" in a class of children of the same age and may become very quiet so that no one notices he is having problems, or he may be overactive so that people will have to notice.

The map pictured in Fig. 15 was used to help a child in an open classroom remember the order of activities. Prior to being given the map, he was always in the wrong place at the wrong time, and he became a discipline problem as a result of everyone relating to him as "in the way." To help him begin the activity, footprints made from construction-paper cutouts were put on the floor of the room—while the children were at recess. (To make these yourself, simply trace around the perimeter of a large shoe.) While the teacher explained the map to the child, she followed the footprints with him several times to make sure he understood what he was supposed to do. The teacher then took up the footprints before the other children came back to class. Clock faces were mounted at each learning station, and corresponding faces were put on the map. With children who cannot tell time, other teachers have used timers, bells, and the flicking of the lights to indicate when a child should change learning stations. (If the child cannot read a clock yet, see the game TIME ON MY HANDS in the next chapter.)

Maps like this can be helpful in any kind of structured situation, including a very traditional class. You must remember, however, that consistency is very important in teaching the impulsive child to conform

65

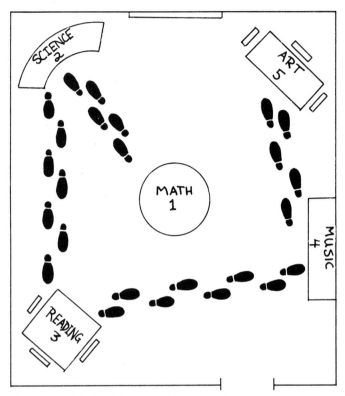

Figure 15 LEARNING CENTER SEQUENCE

to adult expectations. You can't expect a child to learn to follow a schedule if it is always being changed.

Here are the steps you should follow in helping the child use a map to be in the right place at the right time:

1. Put the footprint cutouts on the floor of the room.
2. Walk the child through the correct sequence of directions.
3. Tape clock faces on the tables, desks, or counter tops which show the child what time he should be at each place.
4. Draw a map, like the one in Fig. 15, which shows the footprints and the clocks just as they are arranged in the room.
5. Practice going around the room with the child, using the map as a guide. When the child is used to the routine, take up the footprints and have him use the map alone. Show him how to match up the clocks on the map with the ones on the tables.
6. Finally, remove the clocks that you have mounted around the room. Now the child only has the map to guide him. He should carry it so long as he

feels it is needed. Have extra copies of the map available for the child on
days when he forgets his map.

the secret spy game

Here is an example of a more sophisticated map activity that was
used to help a child and her mother communicate more effectively.
Annie's problem in self-control was more evident in the home than at
school. In fact, while her teacher described her as an angel in class, her
mother said that she was a devil at home because she never listened to
her. Annie and her mother continually bickered over her unwillingness to
clean her room or help around the house. This polarization of Annie's
behavior—good in one place and bad in another—is not uncommon,
and can easily become a fixed and rigid pattern of behavior. The significant adults in the child's life must get together to work out common
solutions to help the child express herself appropriately in any situation.

In this case, at a meeting with the teacher and parents it was
decided to concentrate on trying to help the mother and daughter relate
to each other in a way which would satisfy both their needs. The mother
needed to have some cooperation from her daughter and a sense of
self-respect as a parent. Annie needed more structure in the home to be
able to change her behaviors. As in school, she needed clear assignments
and clear rewards for her good behavior. Both the mother and daughter
needed a way to relate to and communicate with each other which would
be fun and challenging. A map was chosen as a step towards that goal.

Annie's mother played the following SECRET SPY GAME with her
daughter:

1. Draw a map of the child's house, similar to the one shown in Fig. 16,
   which includes each of the rooms where the child must perform chores.
   Make 25 copies of the map.
2. Each day write in two or three chores for the child to do. Locate the
   directions in the room where the chore is to be done.
3. Set a time each day when the child must perform the chores.
4. The adult should hide the map at least an hour before the chore is to be
   done. The map should be hidden in a secret place known only to the child,
   for example, behind a picture or a book.
5. As the child does each chore, he or she should take the map along and
   check off the appropriate box when the chore is complete.
6. Directions for doing the chores may be written in a secret code, as in
   Annie's map, where the last word in the sentence is spelled backwards.

67

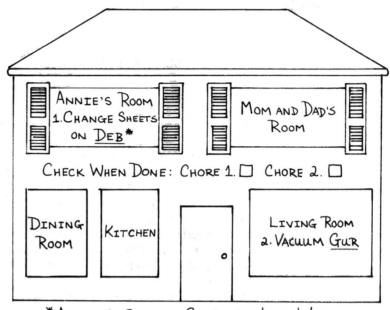

**ANNIE'S SECRET CODE: THE LAST WORD
IN EACH SENTENCE IS SPELLED BACKWARDS**

Figure 16 SPY MAP

7. When all the chores are done for the day, the child should return the map to the secret hiding place.

Annie's mother made twenty-five copies of the map in Fig. 16, leaving out the specific directions so that the chores could be changed. She began playing the SECRET SPY GAME only on Tuesdays and Thursdays, but Annie enjoyed the game so much that by the second week they were playing it every day after school. Her mother was careful to select chores that were not too difficult or time-consuming for Annie.

Annie's spy maps were numbered, and when her mother collected each fifth map (that is, maps 5, 10, 15, 20, and 25), she would place a small surprise for Annie in the secret hiding place. When all twenty-five maps were used, the game ended, and Annie and her mother made a scrapbook from the maps, which they both treasured for some years. Annie continued to do her chores—most of the time—by reading the weekly schedule posted for all family members on the kitchen bulletin board. Through repetition, the chores had become easier for Annie to do, and they became associated with a pleasant game and with the pride that she knew her mother felt. Annie's mother continued to find special treats for her daughter and other activities they could enjoy together.

cooking up new skills

Children love to cook, and judging by the recent publication of at least two dozen children's cookbooks, there are more and more children helping out in the kitchen. It is different, however, for the impulsive child. His level of activity and short attention span make adults wary of putting him in a kitchen, where there are many things for him to "get into" and also many dangers. Still, we must recognize that cooking involves cognitive and behavioral skills that are important for the impulsive child to learn, and it is a high-interest activity that can be done very simply or with a good deal of flare.

I have listed several cookbooks for children in the Suggested Readings, including one which requires no reading. However, I recommend that you make your own recipe cards, which can be geared precisely to your child's needs and abilities. Recipe card 1 (Fig. 17) was made up for a child in the third grade who had a great deal of difficulty in learning math. The math problems presented here were all concepts he was familiar with and could perform without too much difficulty. Recipe card 2 (Fig. 18) was made for a first-grade girl who had very few math or reading skills. Cutouts from newspaper ads were used for the pictures. In both cases, great care was taken to choose the right time and place for the cooking lesson, so that the child would really be free to learn rather than being under the worried eye of an anxious adult.

Figure 17   RECIPE CARD #1

Peanut Butter and Banana Sandwich with Nuts

TO COOK YOU NEED:	1 banana
	2 pieces of bread
	6 cashew nuts
	1 jar of peanut butter
TO EAT YOU NEED:	1 knife
	1 paper plate
	1 napkin
	1 glass of milk
THE MATH YOU NEED TO KNOW:	To count out 6 things
	To count 2 tablespoons
	To divide in 2 (or ½)

69

FIRST: Spread 2 tablespoons of peanut butter on 1 piece of bread.

SECOND: Put 5 pieces of banana on the bread with the peanut butter.

THIRD: Put 6 cashew nuts between the banana slices.

FOURTH: Put the 2 slices of bread together and divide the sandwich into 2 equal halves.

FIFTH: Set the table and EAT.

Figure 18 RECIPE CARD #2: HEALTH SALAD

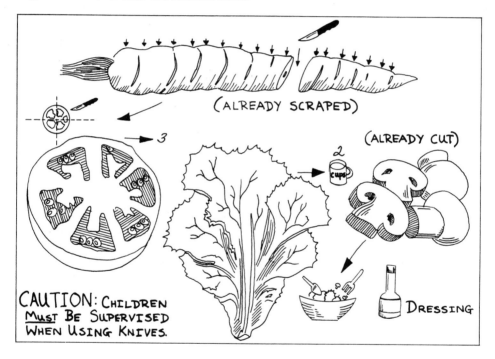

(ALREADY SCRAPED)

(ALREADY CUT)

DRESSING

CAUTION: CHILDREN MUST BE SUPERVISED WHEN USING KNIVES.

6
Slowing down the impulsive child

The passage of time often seems to be subjective. The hours fly by when you are engrossed in a book or an interesting movie, but when you are waiting at the dentist's office to have a cavity filled, minutes move very slowly. Now imagine what the passage of time is like to a child who does not have your experiences or frame of reference, and go on to think about the impulsive child who is hypersensitive to his environment and easily distracted from the demands of the world. Time must seem to pass arbitrarily in spurts and drips—so unpredictably that it might as well be ignored. In fact, complaints about impuslive children frequently focus on behaviors related to their inability to grasp time concepts. They are late coming in from recess or too early going to the next class. They hand in tests before everyone else even though they have not finished them. They rush through meals—or miss them entirely—because they are more interested in something else. And the common threat that underlies these behaviors is that these children are insensitive to the time demands that adults hold to be so important.

This chapter suggests games that will help make the impulsive child more sensitive to the way adults experience time. The impulsive child can be helped to be more aware of his body movements and to be able to control them more. He can learn to use a watch to be on time more often. He can develop a sense of the passage of time. He can begin to understand that acting too quickly may affect his ability to solve problems.

On the other hand, as adults, we must understand that a child's sense of time is an entrenched part of his thinking style, and therefore it may be very difficult to change. And so you must learn to make some allowances for this difference in the impulsive child by looking at the time demands you place on the child, considering whether they are important or merely convenient, and focusing on helping the child understand the need for him to conform to the adult world. The more you see the child's problems with time as skills that he can learn, rather than as just a general rebellion against the adult world, the more support you will be giving to the child in helping him to overcome his difficulties. These games should start you in the right direction.

slow things

SLOW THINGS is a game in which children must practice imitating very slow things such as a turtle, a broken car, a bubble or leaf floating in the air, or a worm. Have the child pantomime the slow thing he likes best, and then have somebody else try to guess what he is miming.

For children who have difficulty imagining themselves as slow things, put on music which has a slow, strong beat, or simply beat a drum more and more slowly, to help the child get a sense of controlling his rhythm. Eventually, however, the child must be able to slow down without an external cue such as music, and to do this he must have an inner sensory image of what it is like to slow down. To see if this activity really has an effect on the child's behavior, ask him to do a chore or some other task the way a turtle or a broken car would do it, and see if he is able to slow down his movements while doing purposeful activities.

guessing time

This is a simple game that will help children to be more aware of time by judging the length of different time intervals. Take a kitchen timer and set it for five minutes. Hide it under a bag or box, and have the child guess when the five minutes are up. The child can use any tricks he needs to help him estimate the time, except of course, another clock. These tricks could include counting or turning on a TV commercial (about 1 minute) or a record (about 2½ minutes). Explore with him other possible ways to help him estimate the passage of time. Here are the rules for the game:

1. Set the timer to 5 minutes, hide it, and say "Go." The child should say "STOP" when he thinks 5 minutes have passed, and you should immediately stop the timer.
2. The child must try to estimate this 5-minute interval for five trials.
3. The child begins the game with 10 points, but he loses a point on each trial for each minute that he overestimates or underestimates the passage of time. For example, if he says stop after only 3 minutes has elasped, he loses two points.
4. Keep a record of the child's estimates on Fig. 19.
5. His final score will indicate his accuracy at estimating time. The higher the score, the better the child's sense of the passage of time. *A score of three points or better wins the game.*

Here is the scoring sheet for Jimmy, who won the game the first time around with the kitchen timer set at five minutes.

Trial No.	Jimmy's Guess	Points
1	7 minutes	8 (he missed by 2 minutes, so he lost 2 points)
2	3 minutes	6 (he missed again by 2, so subtract 2 more)
3	4.5 minutes	5.5 (round to the nearest 0.5 and so subtract 0.5)
4	5 minutes	5.5 (perfect guess; missed only by a few seconds)
5	4 minutes	4.5 (subtract 1 point)

Final Score: 4.5 Jimmy wins!

Figure 19 RECORDING SHEET FOR "GUESSING TIME" GAME *

Trial Number	Child's Guess	Points
1		
2		
3		
4		
5		

*Beginning with 10 points, subtract 1 point for each guess over or under five minutes.

73

If the child likes this game, then it can be repeated with many variations. Have him estimate longer periods of time, such as 15 or 30 minutes, but change the point values so that he doesn't have to guess as accurately for the longer time intervals (for example, let him lose one point for every three minutes he is over or under the actual time). This game is easily (and significantly) incorporated into the child's real world. Have him do his homework or school work for 10 to 15 minutes, stopping when he thinks he is closest to the requested time and writing down the actual time that elapsed. He can do one trial every day, and on Friday he can get a nickel (or other reward) for every session in which he has worked fifteen minutes or over. You'll be astonished at how you can increase the time he spends at his work in just a few weeks.

let the clock beat you

Do you remember the popular TV show "Beat the Clock"? Well, this is the same game in reverse. Instead of having to perform a stunt before the time runs out, the child must *slow down* an 1 *stretch out* the stunt so that he is still doing it when the clock strikes. The purpose of this game is twofold: to reinforce the child's patience while doing a structured activity and to find out what, if anything, keeps the child from concentrating on the activity.

Here is the way to play:

1. Let the child choose an activity that he likes to do while sitting at a table or desk. Suitable activities might include reading a book, working puzzles, drawing dot-to-dot pictures, coloring, and tracing.
2. Explain to the child that he must do the task for 5 minutes. He will start with five points, but every time he looks away he will lose a point.
3. You must sit in back of the child and record each time he looks away. Set a kitchen timer to 5 minutes and say, "Now begin. Take your time and enjoy what you're doing. Don't look away from what you are doing, because I will take one point away each time you look up." Use Fig. 20 to record the child's score.
4. If the child stops the activity before the time rings, he gets no points. If he continues the activity up to the time the buzzer sounds, he gets five points minus the number of times he looked away.
5. When the child makes 20 points (in one session or over several days), he should win a prize. Help him win faster by discussing what things distract him and help him overcome them by either removing the distractions or teaching him to compensate for them.

Figure 20   RECORDING FORM FOR "LET THE CLOCK BEAT YOU"

INSTRUCTIONS: Before beginning the game, enter the level of difficulty that the child has chosen in each of the game's three parts. Do this
by entering the number of points given in each level of difficulty (1, 5, 10
or 25) in columns 2, 3, and 4 for each trial. If the child wins (puts the
correct number of pegs in to answer the math problem before the time
runs out), then enter the total score in the last column. If he does not meet
any of these requirements, enter "0."

Trial Number	Point Value for Pegs	Point Value for Math Problems	Point Value for Clock	Total Points
1				
2				
3				
4				
5				
6				
7				
8				

Total Score _____

Note: The child may play the game as many times as he likes to win 100 points, within one
session. If he quits or goes to something else, then he must start the next time with a
new recording sheet and no points.

Here are some common things that distract children from working
and some hints on methods to help children overcome these distractions:

Visual Distractions

People walking by	Use work booths which cut off the view of other people.
Too many things on the desk	The child should only have on his desk what he is working with at the time.
Windows	Have the child's back to the window or use curtains.
Unusual wall or floor patterns	Keep wall decorations simple around the area where the child must work.
Bright colors	Use muted and pastel colors.

75

Sound Distractions

Traffic noises
Noise from other children
Household noises
TV
Radio

Do everything you can to keep the working environment quiet. If this is impossible, you may try two different approaches: cut out all noises with earphones that are not hooked up, or introduce a competing noise which will drown out the distracting noise and will relax or soothe the child. The competing noise might be soft music or a low buzzing sound (called *white noise*). This second approach will not work with all children, and you should be careful that it does not become a distraction itself.

If you find that any of these techniques help in getting the child to concentrate more, make sure to share them with other people who work with the child so that he may have the benefit of a controlled environment at home and in other classes.

time on your hands

As I have said, impulsive children frequently are in the wrong place at the wrong time. The obvious solution to this seems to be to teach them to wear and read a watch, but this not quite as easy as it sounds. First, it is difficult for many impulsive children to tell time. Children with learning problems often find the number system of time confusing, have a hard time differentiating the long and the short hand, and may even experience directional problems, forgetting which way the hands rotate. Then there is the problem of keeping the watch. Impulsive children are renowned for their ability to lose almost anything, anytime, anywhere, and few parents are willing to replace even the most inexpensive watch more than once. Finally, there is the problem of getting the child to pay attention to the watch even when he wears it. Wearing a watch doesn't necessarily make adults arrive on time when they should, so why should it work better with children?

The TIME ON YOUR HANDS game focuses on the three major problems that the children have in wearing a watch: how to read it correctly, how to avoid losing it, and how to use it effectively.

For this game, you will need to purchase a digital watch, which can be bought for $9 to $12. These watches come in many styles and you should purchase one that the child will really like. A digital watch is recommended over a traditional one with hands because it is easier for most children to understand. Before the child is given the watch, however, he must demonstrate that he can tell time to at least a minimum degree. Explain the basic facts to the child, and then give the quiz shown on Fig. 21. He must get 100 percent on the quiz before you proceed. Use Fig. 22 to review basic time facts.

1. What does your watch look like when you eat your breakfast?

2. Circle the time that is closer to your bedtime.

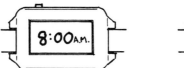 

3. What does your watch look like when you have recess?

4. What will this watch look like when one more minute passes?

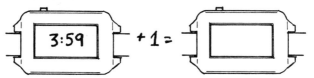

5. Circle the time that is closer to your dinnertime.

6. What does your watch look like at the following times?

Dinnertime   Bedtime

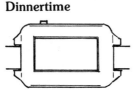 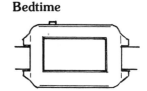

Time for homework   Time school starts

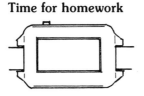

Figure 21   "TIME ON YOUR HANDS" QUIZ

1. There are 60 minutes in an hour.
   The minutes are shown on the right of the two dots.

2. There are 24 hours in the day, but the numbers on the left only go up to 12.
   The hours are shown on the left of the two dots.

3. After 60 minutes, the hour changes by one number and the minutes go back to zero.

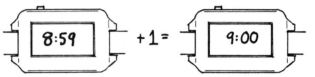

4. The first 12 hours are called "AM," and begin at midnight and last until noon.

5. The numbers then start over and the next 12 hours in the afternoon and evening are called "PM."

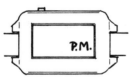

Some important times to know are:

Your bedtime

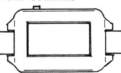

Time for school

Mealtimes

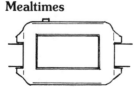

Time for homework

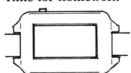

Figure 22
BASIC TIME FACTS
(For a Digital Watch)

KEEPING THE WATCH ON

Although there is no foolproof way to keep a child from losing a watch when he is really intent on doing so, here is a trick that works most of the time. Punch two extra holes in the watchband using an awl or sharp knife on the side of the band with the buckle on it. Children's watchbands are usually made of plastic, and you should not have too much trouble doing this. Then at the beginning of the day, attach the watch to the child's shirt sleeve using safety pins just large enough to fit past the band. The smaller the pins you use, the more difficult it will be for the child to remove them. If the child takes off his shirt during the day, the watch should be unbuckled, but the safety pins should not be removed, and the watch must come off with the shirt. For warm days when it is not practical for the child to wear a long-sleeved shirt, an alternative method is to have him wear the watch as a pocket watch, pinning a strong piece of material to the child's watchband and the other end to his belt loop or waistband. The child will then carry the watch in his pocket rather than wearing it on his wrist. Again, you must put the safety pins into the watchband and into the clothing so that they are comfortable but difficult for the child to remove.

TIME ON YOUR HANDS is an easy game to play, directly addressing the problem of having the child be where he is supposed to be on time. Pick three places that are most important for the child to be on time. These might be at the breakfast table, his desk at school, and his bed at bedtime. Now, at each of these places, tape on a drawing of the digital watch (such as the ones shown in Figs. 21 and 22, with the correct time the child is supposed to be there. The object of the game is to be at the drawing at the exact time that the watch changes to display the same "face" as the one on the drawing. When the child is at the right place at the right time, he gets a point (see Fig. 23 for the score sheet). He must be at each drawing *exactly* when the face on his watch matches the face on the drawing, or he gets no point. Being early doesn't count, because the child could wander away again. An adult must also be there to record the point. This is not only to keep the game accurate, but also to get the child involved in an appropriate activity—which is the real purpose of the game. For instance, a child might be able to show up at his desk at the right time after recess, but he must also learn to get right to work instead of continuing to play. His teacher should be at the desk to give him the point and to encourage him to begin his work again. Similarly, being in bed at 9:00 does not mean the child is necessarily going to go right to sleep. Rather the adult should require the child to be undressed and washed before the time when he must match his watch face to the digital watch drawing on the bedpost.

The child will be able to earn a maximum of 21 points per week, the exact number depending on how many of the checkpoints are at

Figure 23 RECORDING SHEET FOR "TIME ON YOUR HANDS"

INSTRUCTIONS: Use one recording sheet for each week that you play the game. Put a check mark in the appropriate box each time the child is at the right place at the right time.

Write in the place the child should be	*Write in the time the child should be there*	*Put a check each day he or she is there on time*						
		M	T	W	Th	F	Sa	Sun
1. _____	_____	__	__	__	__	__	__	__
2. _____	_____	__	__	__	__	__	__	__
3. _____	_____	__	__	__	__	__	__	__

Total checks
for the week _____

school (where, of course, he doesn't go during the weekend). Whatever the possible total number is, give the child a small reward when he earns 25 percent of the possible points, give him a medium reward when he earns 50 percent of the possible points, and give him something really special if he can be in the right place at the right time 75 percent of the time (for example, if he earns 15 out of 20 possible points). Continue the game until the child can earn 75 percent or better for two consecutive weeks.

the problem, the peg, and the clock

The activities that have been presented so far in this section have been aimed at changing the nature of the way the impulsive child relates to time. If the previous activities have been successful, the child you are working with has developed some new skills in learning to control his movements, in estimating time intervals, and in learning to concentrate. The present activity combines all these skills and adds one more—the skill of assessing his own strengths and weaknesses. The successful completion of this activity will have a profound impact on the child you are working with, which you should acknowledge. It will mean that he has gained control over the complex relationships among his mind, his body, and the expectations of the outside world. It will mean that the child has made specific *choices* to try and modify his behavior, and with your help he has succeeded. Those of you with a more theoretical or technical orientation may also find this game useful as a diagnostic tool and a way to keep track of the progress that children make.

This activity may seem a little complex to you at first, but this is because it is designed to measure a complex interaction of skills. The child must do three things at once to play the game: (1) solve a math problem, (2) put that number of pegs in a pegboard which corresponds to the correct answer to the problem, and (3) estimate how long it will take to carry out the first two steps. Each step has four levels of difficulty: (1) "a cinch," (2) "easy," (3) "hard," and (4) "a tough one." When the child completes the task correctly (that is, puts the correct number of pegs in the board before the time runs out), then he will win a specified number of points based on the level of difficulty he has preselected for each part of the game (the problem, the peg, and the clock). This will become clearer as you construct the game.

THE PROBLEMS

Make 48 math flash cards, using 3 × 5 index cards with the problem on one side and the answer on the back. Divide the cards into four sets of 12 cards each so that one set consists of problems that you know the child can do (cinch); one set consists of problems that the child has had but makes some errors on (easy); one set consists of problems that the child has more difficulty with (hard); and one set consists of problems that the child has just learned to do and so should be very difficult for him (tough). Figure 24 (see p. 82) shows a sample sheet of problems prepared for a first grader. When the child plays the game, the cinch problems will each be worth 1 point to him, the easy problems will be worth 5 points, the hard problems will be worth 10 points, and the tough problems will be worth 25 points.

THE PEGS

The pegs are also divided into four difficulty levels, based on size and ease of manipulation. This will be an important factor for children with poor finger control but will also have significance for other children playing the game. The easier the pegs are to grasp, the lower the point value they have, and this can make a difference for any child when under pressure.

Figure 25 (see p. 83) shows you the recommended ways to make the pegs as well as the pegboard. The level of difficulty of each type of peg will have the same point scores as the math problems: cinch 1; easy 5; hard 10; and tough 25.

81

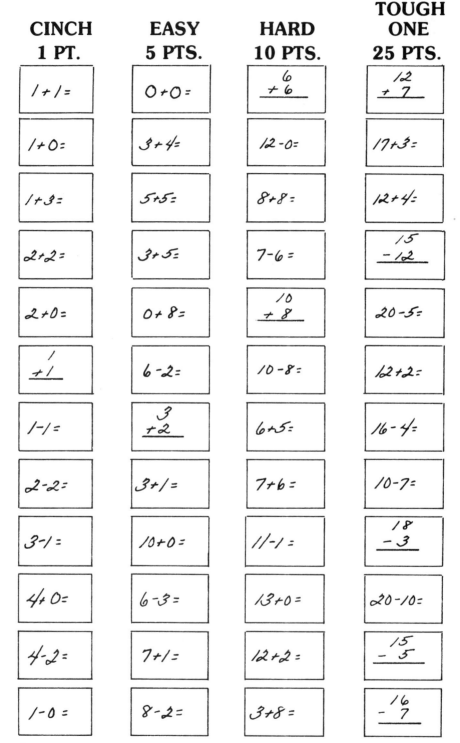

CINCH 1 PT.	EASY 5 PTS.	HARD 10 PTS.	TOUGH ONE 25 PTS.
1 + 1 =	0 + 0 =	$\begin{array}{r} 6 \\ + 6 \\ \hline \end{array}$	$\begin{array}{r} 12 \\ + 7 \\ \hline \end{array}$
1 + 0 =	3 + 4 =	12 - 0 =	17 + 3 =
1 + 3 =	5 + 5 =	8 + 8 =	12 + 4 =
2 + 2 =	3 + 5 =	7 - 6 =	$\begin{array}{r} 15 \\ - 12 \\ \hline \end{array}$
2 + 0 =	0 + 8 =	$\begin{array}{r} 10 \\ + 8 \\ \hline \end{array}$	20 - 5 =
$\begin{array}{r} 1 \\ + 1 \\ \hline \end{array}$	6 - 2 =	10 - 8 =	12 + 2 =
1 - 1 =	$\begin{array}{r} 3 \\ + 2 \\ \hline \end{array}$	6 + 5 =	16 - 4 =
2 - 2 =	3 + 1 =	7 + 6 =	10 - 7 =
3 - 1 =	10 + 0 =	11 - 1 =	$\begin{array}{r} 18 \\ - 3 \\ \hline \end{array}$
4 + 0 =	6 - 3 =	13 + 0 =	20 - 10 =
4 - 2 =	7 + 1 =	12 + 2 =	$\begin{array}{r} 15 \\ - 5 \\ \hline \end{array}$
1 - 0 =	8 - 2 =	3 + 8 =	$\begin{array}{r} 16 \\ - 7 \\ \hline \end{array}$

Figure 24

THE CLOCK

Make a clock similar to the one shown in Fig. 25, dividing it into four quarters. As you can see, each section of the clock stands for a different time interval. The time interval indicates how long the child will have to solve the math problem. Naturally, the smaller the time interval, the more

Figure 25 THE PROBLEM, THE PEG, AND THE CLOCK

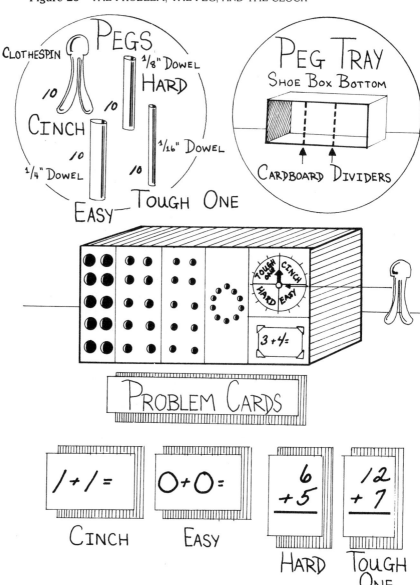

difficult the game. As in the other steps, there are four levels of difficulty, the five-minute interval being a cinch (1 point); the 3-minute interval being easy (5 points); the 1-minute interval being hard (10 points); and the half-minute interval being tough (25 points). Use a kitchen timer to time the child for each trial.

PLAYING THE GAME

Once you are set up, the game itself is quite simple. The child begins by selecting the level of difficulty that he wishes to play at for each of the three parts of the game. Explain to him how he will accumulate points depending on what levels he picks, and that he must satisfy all three parts of the game (that is, get the correct number of pegs in the board to solve the math problem before the clock runs out) in order to win each round. First he should select which pile of cards to choose a problem from. Next he should decide which size pegs he will use, and he should set them out close to him. Finally, he should decide how long he thinks he will need to play the game, and he should set the clock dial accordingly. The child must obtain 100 points in one sitting, playing the game as many times as he likes, to win a prize.

Now you are ready to begin. Set the timer for the time interval that the child has selected and say "Go." The child should take any card from the problem deck that he has selected and try to solve it in his head (pencil and paper may be allowed, but it is preferable not to use them, for they may slow the child down so much that he will not be able to complete the task in time). When the child thinks he has the right answer, he must put the number of pegs in the board that correspond to what he thinks is the correct solution. If he does not have all the pegs in before the clock runs out, then he gets no points. Also, if the answer is wrong, he gets no points (the answer is on the back of the cards). Use Fig. 26 as a recording sheet for each game.

The child's success in winning points will largely depend on how well he assesses his math ability, his fine motor skills, and his speed. If he sets his goals too high in any one of these areas, he will not get points. On the other hand, if he sets his goals too low in all areas, he will earn points at a very slow pace, and it may be impossible for him to earn 100 points at one sitting.

It is *your* task to help the child find out what are his strengths and weaknesses and how he can make the most of his strengths. Every time the child completes the task, whether he gets the right answer or not, talk to him about his performance and help him to see how he can increase his point scoring (for example, by selecting harder pegs, harder problems, or shorter time intervals), or what he can do to avoid failure.

Because this game calls for the child to use several new skills at once, motivation is an extremely important factor. If he can earn the 100

Figure 26 RECORDING FORM FOR "THE PROBLEM, THE PEG, AND THE CLOCK"

	MATH PROBLEM			PEGS			CLOCK			
	Point Value	Right	Wrong	Point Value	Right	Wrong	Point Value	Right	Wrong	Total
Trial 1										
Trial 2										
Trial 3										
Trial 4										
Trial 5										
Trial 6										
Trial 7										
Trial 8										
Trial 9										
Trial 10										
Trial 11										
Trial 12										
Trial 13										
Trial 14										
Trial 15										

INSTRUCTIONS: Enter the point values that the child has selected for each of the three parts of the game, before he begins each trial. Score the math part right if the child knows the correct answer; score the peg part right if the correct number of pegs are placed in the board; and score the clock part right if both of these previous things are done within the alloted time. If *all three* parts of the game are scored "right," then enter the combined point values in the Total column. The child wins the game when he gets 100 points in one sitting.

points in one sitting, then he should get a really terrific prize. And *you* should also get a special prize for your role in helping the child reach his goal. Set aside some special money or time to reward yourself. Explain to the child that if he wins, then you win, and you will both be more motivated to find ways to win this game.

7 Learning to think before you act

One theory about childhood impulsivity states that children without self-control have a mediational language deficit and do not use language concepts to regulate and monitor their own behavior. In simpler terms, this theory suggests that the impulsive child does not think before he acts in the same way that other children his age do, even though he has the ability to do so.* The average child, from age five or six, will reflect on most new things before acting, planning how he will respond and attempting to see at least the initial steps toward the solution before going ahead and attempting to solve the problem. The impulsive child, on the other hand, lacks these skills. When he sees a new problem, he forges ahead, and more often than not will make a mistake because he has not taken the time to look at just what steps he should take. The impulsive child locks himself into an answer too early, as if he were a racehorse blindly heading for the finish line. The reflective child, on the other hand, heads toward a solution the way a jumper negotiates a steeplechase: estimating distances, keeping his strength in reserve, and accommodating his actions to the demands of each obstacle.

*The activities in this section *assume* that the child has the ability to reflect on what he does; however, not all children possess this ability. Some children who mature late may not develop this ability until they are eleven or twelve or older. Some children with minimal or moderate brain damage may lack the ability to reflect throughout their lives. However they will develop other compensatory ways to solve problems. To assess whether a child has the capacity to reflect (that is, to plan, evaluate, reason, judge, use insight), you should have him tested by a qualified psychologist.

Can an impulsive child learn to be reflective and think before he acts? Can a racehorse run a steeplechase? In most cases, given the right training and guidance, the answer is yes. (See Donald Meichenbaum's *Cognitive Behavior Modification* listed in the Suggested Reading section for a state-of-the-art survey of current research on teaching new thinking patterns.)

Mazes are often used as a way to measure impulsivity in children because they allow us to miniaturize the world and look at the child's problem on a smaller scale. When presented with a maze, the impulsive child typically reacts very quickly and immediately begins the maze, paying very little attention to which way the paths go. The impulsive child typically enters blind alleys, cuts corners, wanders with his pencil, and is sloppy in his work. In contrast, the reflective child examines the maze before beginning, stays within the path, and enters fewer blind alleys because he looks ahead before making a choice, and he takes an organized, evaluative approach to the maze rather than relying on trial and error.

The first four games in this chapter use mazes to teach the impulsive child to think and consider alternatives before he acts. The ultimate goal is to teach the child to slow down and analyze problems before attempting them. The activities begin concretely and gradually force the child to develop the skills necessary to consider each step of the problem-solving process individually. The ONE MORE TIME MAZE game introduces a thinking-out-loud technique (developed by Bonnie Camp of the University of Colorado School of Medicine, Donald Meichenbaum of the University of Waterloo, and others), which is used as a basis for teaching the child more reflective thought processes. The game THINKING NUMBERS OUT LOUD extends this approach to help the child reduce his impulsivity in solving arithmetic problems. Because each activity builds on the skills developed in the preceding ones, it is recommended that the child do each one in sequence.

a-maze me

To begin this series of activities, you must teach the child to "run" a three-dimensional maze with the correct path already marked. Take a large shallow box approximately 2 ft × 2 ft × 3 in. deep and cut out a piece of light-colored construction paper that will fit neatly into the bottom. Now, choose one of the four mazes from Fig. 27, using your child's chronological age as a guide. If your child has difficulty in school, then choose a maze at a lower age level. It is better to choose a maze that is too easy rather than one that is too hard. You can always change the

87

Figure 27

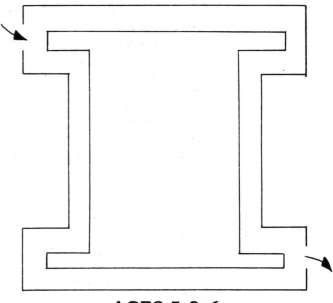

AGES 5 & 6

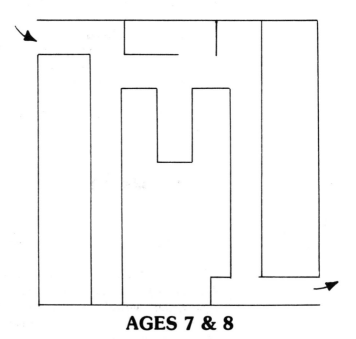

AGES 7 & 8

Figure 27   (continued)

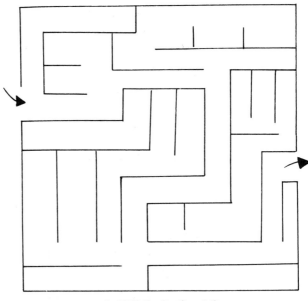

AGES 9 & 10

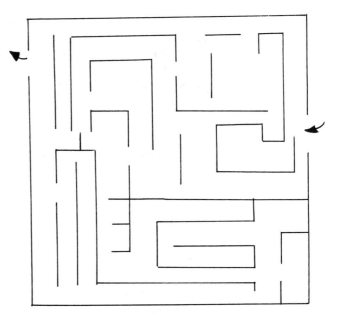

AGES 11 & 12

maze, but you should avoid making the child feel like a failure because he cannot do what you expect him to do.

Copy an enlarged version of the maze that you have selected onto the construction paper, and glue the paper onto the bottom of the box. Then cut out pieces of yellow ribbon and tack them onto the bottom of the box, so that the pieces show the shortest route to the end of the maze. Finally, cut out three blue squares and three red circles and tack them at various places along the ribbon route. Place a small doll, dressed to represent the same sex as the child, next to the maze box. Now you are ready to begin.

Sit with the child on the floor. Set him up so that he can comfortably run the doll through the maze. Then say, "I want your doll to solve this maze. Start at the beginning at the word GO and follow the yellow ribbon until your doll comes to the end. **When you come to a red circle, you must say 'Hop three times slowly,' and your doll must hop three times. When you come to a blue square, you must say 'Do two slow somersaults', and your doll must turn around twice in the air.** When you finish the maze, you will get five chips. When you get 40 chips, you will get a special prize."

The rationale behind this activity is that the child can concentrate on the intermediate steps to the goal (responding correctly to the red and blue shapes) because the solution is clearly marked for him. Because there is no pressure on him to solve the problem correctly, there will be less chance that he will act impulsively. It is important to make sure that the child reacts appropriately to the red circles and blue squares, and you should encourage him to say the words and do the actions slowly and clearly. While he does not get penalized in this activity if he skips a circle or square or forgets to say the right words, he will get points taken off for this in the next game.

a-maze me again

Using the same maze that you constructed for the last game, take up the yellow ribbon, replace the circles and squares, and say, "Now I want you to run the same maze again, but this time it will be harder because I've taken up the ribbon, and you will have to find the way out by yourself. If you can do this, you will get ten chips each time you run the maze correctly. However, you must whisper to yourself 'Hop three times slowly,' and your doll must do this when you come to a blue square. You must whisper 'Do two slow somersaults' when you come to a red circle, and your doll must do this also. If your doll forgets to hop or somersault in the right place, you will not win any points."

90

Having the child whisper the correct response at the intermediate steps of the maze is in itself an intermediate step in teaching the child to use his silent thoughts to control his actions.

After the child has run the race correctly without the ribbon to guide him, explain that if he can run the maze without going into any blind alleys he will get a bonus of 5 points for each maze he completes correctly (a total of 15 points for each maze). To help the child win these extra points, tack down a STOP, LOOK, AND THINK cue card, such as the one shown in Fig. 28, at each intersection where the child has previously taken the wrong direction. When he comes to a cue card, he should whisper, "Stop, look ahead, and think," before proceeding.

Figure 28

If the cue cards do not help the child and he consistently gets lost in the maze, then tack the yellow ribbon back down to show him the shortest route. Also retack the circles and squares on the top of the ribbon. Help the child accept the fact that he needs these additional cues (that is, the ribbon and the Stop, Look, and Think card,) and he can still win the game when he earns 40 points. However, he only gets five points each time he completes the maze when the ribbon is down.

the one-more-time maze

In this activity, we will begin to see whether the child can expand his ability to use language to help control his impulsivity. To review: in the previous two games, the child has learned to whisper directions to himself

91

which remind him to perform unrelated steps to a goal (hopping and somersaulting while solving the maze puzzle). In theory, the child can learn to think before he acts if he is first taught to think out loud, whisper the same words, and finally say these directions silently as an automatic response to approaching a problem. This is called internal speech. This method has been used effectively with several groups of impulsive and hyperactive children to increase their ability to solve problems correctly. It is based on the way most children develop self-guiding speech to the point where they can eventually have a complete internal dailogue with themselves.

Select a maze from Fig. 27 which is more difficult than the one you chose for the last game and enlarge it so that it fits into the shallow box that you used. If the child was using the ten- to twelve-year maze, then you can make up your own more difficult maze, or use one from one of the maze books listed in the Suggested Readings section. Give the child the doll again and say, "Now I want you to have your doll solve a more difficult maze. There are more traps here, so you must whisper to yourself '*Stop, look, and think*' every time you come to an intersection where you have a decision to make. You will get 15 points every time you can complete the maze, *but every time you go into a blind alley you will have 5 points deducted*. When you go into a blind alley and come out of it I'll place a Stop, Look, and Think card there so that you won't make the same mistake twice." Time the child with a stopwatch the first time he tries the maze. When the child runs the maze the second time, have him say stop, look and think, whenever he comes to a card that you have placed on the board. (He should pause for at least five seconds before proceeding and should trace ahead with his eyes.) If he continually makes the wrong choices, even though there is a card to remind him to think before he acts, then you must teach him how to evaluate his choices through the thinking-out-loud technique.

The thinking out loud technique is used to help the child develop a pattern of analyzing choices rather than using trial and error. While this technique can theoretically be used to help a child solve any type of age-appropriate problem, it has been most thoroughly researched with visual-motor problems such as mazes.

The method is based on the assumption that children can learn to imitate the thought processes that adults use to analyze problems by repeating the key phrases involved. As the child practices solving problems and repeating these key phrases aloud, he should develop an association between these thought patterns and similar types of problems—just as he learns other behavior patterns. The technique is presented in the following steps:

92

1. The adult performs the problem that the child is having trouble with, *thinking out loud* as he works.

2. The child does the same problem, repeating the key phrases that the adult has used.

3. The child solves the same problem again, this time repeating the key phrase in a whisper.

4. The child solves the same problem a third time, this time saying the key phrase silently to himself.

As an example, in one study teenage girls were taught to use this method to help themselves with a weight problem. The adult would sit down with one girl at a time in front of a table of food high in protein or high in starch. The adult said something like "I have a choice to make: to eat the food that is nutritious and nonfattening, or to eat food that will make me feel badly about myself. I won't fool myself this time; I shall eat what is good for me." Then the girl said the same phrases aloud and ate the food high in protein. She whispered the phrase again, and ate more protein. She said the phrase a third time, again eating the protein and refusing the starchy foods. The girls were encouraged to think these exact same thoughts again and to remember that they could make the right choices each time they were tempted to eat foods high in starch.

In learning to solve mazes by analyzing them, the child should go through the following procedure:

1. The adult should run the maze up to the point where the child had trouble. He should think aloud as he goes, saying simple phrases such as ***"Now I must make a decision. I must slow down to do this. I must look ahead before I enter an alley. I must follow the path first with my eyes. Then I will go ahead."*** The adult should finish the maze using these phrases at each intersection where a choice is necessary. Remember that the intersections where the child had difficulty before will be marked with a Stop, Look, and Think cue card.

2. The child should then run the maze using the doll, repeating aloud the same phrases that the adult used each time he comes to a cue card. When he completes the maze he gets 15 points if he has not gone into any blind alleys (5 points are deducted each time he goes into a blind alley).

3. The child should then run the maze a second time, but now he should whisper the phrases when he comes to the cue cards. The same point system applies.

4. Finally, the child should run the maze saying the phrases to himself when he comes to the cue cards. The same point system applies.

5. As a final test of whether the child has learned to run the maze correctly using the thinking-out-loud technique, have him run the maze one last time, about four days later without cue cards. Time him with a stopwatch. He should be able to run the maze with very few errors, and he should show signs of analyzing the maze as he goes (pausing at difficult intersections, moving his lips as he thinks to himself). Compare his time on the maze to the first time he ran it. If it is *slower,* and the child makes fewer mistakes, then you can assume that he has learned some new intellectual process which helped him reach his goal.

Remember that there will be some children who cannot benefit from the thinking-out-loud technique. They may have trouble remembering the phrases that you have identified for them, or the problem you have asked them to solve may be too difficult. If the child experiences continual frustration with the maze you have chosen for him, switch to an easier maze so that he may experience success. Be sensitive to every way in which the child shows that he can control his actions, and reinforce these behaviors every time they occur.

a-mazing homework

If the child has enjoyed the preceding maze activities, you can encourage this interest by giving him mazes for homework, in which he can demonstrate his ability to solve problems and control his impulsivity. There are many books on mazes available for children (see the Suggested Readings section) which are popular with children at all skill levels. Choose a book at the appropriate skill level of your child and have him select ten mazes that he would like to do. Explain to him that not only are you interested in having him get to the end of each maze, but that you want him to show you that he can solve the maze *in his mind* before he does it with the pencil (you want him to think about what he is doing before he acts).

Give the child a maze to do for homework and have him bring it to you when he is finished. Say that he will get 20 points for each maze, but that he will get points deducted for things that show he has not thought about what he is doing. When he has 150 points, he will win a prize.

Figure 29 shows you how to score the homework. Make ten copies of this score sheet so that you have one for each maze. Figure 30 shows you how a sample maze was scored.

Figure 29 SCORE SHEET FOR A-MAZING HOMEWORK

Maze No.	Start with 20 points	Subtract 1 point for each cut corner	Subtract 1 point for each line that is crossed	Subtract 1 point for each blind alley that is entered	Total for each maze
1					
2					
3					
4					
5					
6					
7					
8					
9					
10					
11					
12					
13					
14					
15					

Total Points _____
(when 150 points is reached, the child wins)

thinking numbers out loud

While mazes are a good way to look at children's problem-solving styles and abilities and to train them toward more effective ways to handle decisions, the real test is to see if they can be less impulsive in solving school problems.

Take the math cards you used in the game THE PROBLEM, THE PEG, AND THE CLOCK. If you have not done this activity, then make up a deck of at least 24 math cards ranging from problems that are very easy for the child to ones that are difficult (see Fig. 24, for examples). Put the answer to each problem on the back of the card. Shuffle the deck, give the child a plain sheet of paper, and place one of the cards on top of the paper. Ask the child to solve the problem, and when he is through turn over the card

Figure 30

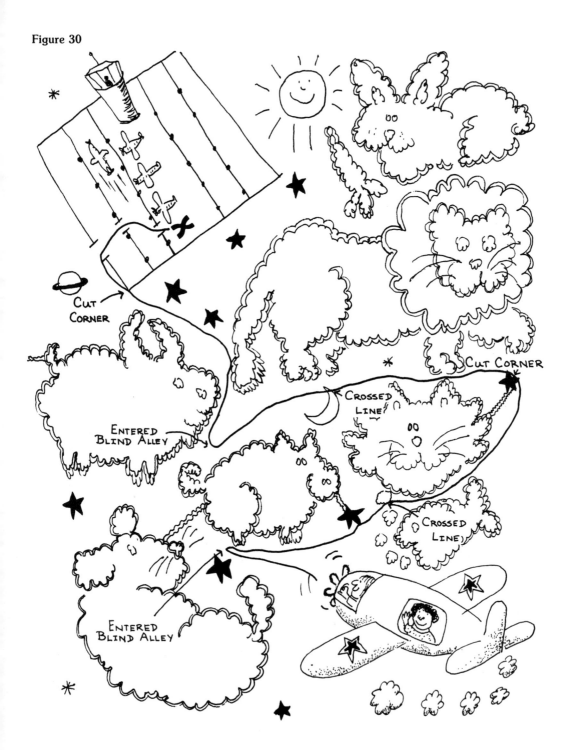

to see if the answer is right. If it is right, give him praise and write a score of three points on the paper. If it is wrong, turn the card back over, and place a Stop, Look and Think card (*see* Fig. 28,) next to the problem card, saying "Now I want you to try thinking aloud as you solve the problem. Just say whatever you are thinking." If the child gets the right answer the second time he tries the problem, give him two points on the paper and go on to the next card in the deck. If he gets it wrong, say "Let me do the problem for you, showing you how I think out loud. Listen carefully, because I will want you to say the same things that I say." Then proceed to solve the problem, thinking out loud in simple short phrases. Here is an example:

$$\begin{array}{r} 23 \\ -7 \\ \hline \end{array}$$

Problem: 23
           −7

"This is a subtraction problem."

"The first step is to take 7 away from 3."

"But, since 7 is larger than three it is a *borrowing problem*."

(*Note:* it is helpful to categorize "types" of problems.)

"So we must *borrow* 10 from the '2' column." (put a 1 by the 3)

"This leaves 1 in the '2' column." (show with your pencil)

"Now we have 13 minus 7."

"The answer is 6." (write the answer)

"Now we have 1 minus 0."

"That is 1." (write the answer)

"The answer is 16."

Then say, "Okay, now I want you to try to solve the same problem, thinking out loud the way I did. We are going to tape-record what you say to make sure that you are going through all the right steps. If you get the answer correct on the third try, you will get one point. Remember 10 points in this game win a prize."

Tape-record the child as he solves the problem out loud. If he gets the problem wrong at this point, play the tape back and write down each thing that the child said. Analyze the way the child approached the problem, and look for the steps he skipped or where other obvious bits of information are lacking. For example, here is the way that Gloria, aged eight, and Peter, aged nine, solved the same problem.

I have made comments about their thought processes and what

97

they imply. You should do a similar analysis, possibly with consultation from a math specialist.

Gloria said:	*Comments*
"This is a subtraction problem. It means to borrow. Three take away 7 equals, uh, you have to borrow. Uh, let's see—3 minus 7, 3 minus 7, uh, I don't know."	She correctly identifies the problem. She correctly identifies the computational process. She does not know how to do the calculation, so you must reteach this skill. She is, of course, just guessing. Rather than guess, she should be taught to think out loud the phrase, "I don't understand this. I must ask for help rather than guess."

Peter said:	
"Uh, oh, borrowing again, huh? Let's see 3 borrow from 2 and that's 13. Now let's see, 13 minus 7 equals 6 and bring down your 2, here. That's 26. That's your answer.	Peter made a mistake right off due to his impulsivity. He did not cross out the 2 and write in 1 and so he brought down the wrong number. He should think out loud the phrase: "I will work more slowly and use my pencil to do each step."

To review, here are the steps to the THINKING NUMBERS GAME.

1. Give the child a problem card and a blank piece of paper.
2. If he solves the problem right, he gets three points.
3. If he gets the wrong answer, have him think out loud and try again.
4. If he gets the right answer now, he gets two points. Mark it on the paper.
5. If he gets the wrong answer again, you must do the problem for him, thinking out loud as you work.
6. Have him try the problem again, trying to copy your thoughts. Tape-record his thoughts and then transcribe the tape. Analyze the problem with him, identifying the points where he makes mistakes. If he gets the right answer, he gets one point. If he is wrong, give him 1 point for trying, and work on the specific problems he shows.
7. Select another problem from the deck and begin again. Because you have shuffled a deck of very easy to difficult cards, he should be able to win 10 points eventually, even though he will not be able to master every single problem. When he wins 10 points he should get a prize.

This game may take several sessions to play, so remind yourself of the purpose each time you play: the child must learn to think about his approach to each problem, to analyze his mistakes, and to avoid repeating them. He must learn to use language as a key to focusing his attention on the problem. This is the key to success!

8

Learning
to obey rules

To many people, the child who is most difficult to understand is the one child in the class or the family who does not follow the rules that everyone else does. It is difficult to say why a child does not do what we expect of him; however, blaming the child or writing him off as spoiled or stubborn is of little help to anyone. Let's assume instead that the child has not yet learned all the cognitive skills he needs to obey rules. These include: comprehending the rule, remembering the rule, knowing when the rule applies and when it doesn't, understanding why the rule should be followed, and forming a concept of the importance of rules in general. The child with a learning disability will have a difficult time with many of these skill areas. The child who is a management problem may not have the motivation to learn to use one or all of these skills, or he may simply have not had the opportunity to learn them in a supportive way.

The activities in this section give the child opportunities to help practice the skills he needs to follow rules. They will also help the adult working with him to realize just where the problem lies. Because the activities are fun, they will be self-motivating for the child, and because they are presented in game format, they can be practiced over and over again.

But before we begin, here is a game for you to play which will help you think about whether or not your expectations for the child's rules are realistic. Sometimes we are arbitrary about the rules we give a child or how we enforce them. Sometimes the rules which we emphasize so

99

much to our children do not reflect our true values or the behaviors that are most important to us. Our own confusion and inconsistencies can be a big part of the problem. So, give this game your full attention and see what you find out about yourself. You may be surprised.

the perfect child game

This is a game of self-exploration. It is simple, but you have to play it honestly for it to be of value. Sit down by yourself with a piece of paper, a pencil, and a watch with a seconds hand. Now write at the top of the paper the incomplete sentence "I want a child who . . ."

Now, complete the sentence as many times as you can in one minute, writing down each phrase on a separate line. Are you ready? Go.

Now let's look back at your answers. Did any of them surprise you? When you let your mind go and you must think quickly, sometimes you come up with answers you never would have thought of, but these may be closer to your real values and priorities than you realize. For instance, when I did this exercise I wrote:

I want a child who:
is respectful
listens to me
is happy
is free and creative
is bright
is warm and loving
has good values

Although the sentence is phrased in the abstract, in this kind of a game we always assume people are basing their wishes for a "perfect" child on their own child. You can see that the first two things that occurred to me were that I wanted my little girl to be well behaved. This is important to me. Then I wanted her to enjoy her childhood, to be happy, free, creative, and bright. Finally, I wanted her to have good feelings about herself and others and to be able to express them.

If I had had more time and had thought about what I was writing, I probably would have put down the same things but reversed their order. I was surprised to see that concern about my little girl's behavior occurred to me before anything else (by the way, she is very well behaved).

When I give this exercise to the parents of very difficult children, they tend to put down predominantly negative statements (for example, I

100

want a child who . . . does *not* talk back, does *not* misbehave, does *not* run around). The more they make statements that are solely concerned with the child's welfare rather than with their own convenience (for example, I want a child who is . . . strong, healthy, happy, and so forth), the less serious I judge the problem. When parents wish for a perfect child, they reflect the values they want their children to have and the behaviors that are important to them on a day-to-day basis. At best, we can hope for a balance between what we want a child to be and what the child can be.

The purpose of this game is to see what your priorities are for your child's values and behaviors (as revealed by your quick uncensored responses) and whether they are realistic. Are your expectations reasonable? Are you wishing for a perfect child, rather than for one who is more independent and in control? Do you want things that are contradictory? Do you expect even more of your child than you do of yourself? There is no such thing as a perfect parent and there is no such thing as a perfect child. Rather, parents and children must find a middle ground where they can be good enough for each other. And in this middle ground exist their rules for living.

the rules contract

Before working on the cognitive skills involved in rule learning, I recommend that you begin with a tried and true behavioral approach to child management, the *behavioral contract.* The subsequent games in this chapter will be most effective when a contract exists between the child and the adult which makes it clear that they are united in a common venture. The RULES CONTRACT (see Fig. 31) sets forth exactly which rules you would like the child to learn and what he will get if he learns them. In the sample I have provided, we expected Harold to learn four rules in a month's period, one new rule each week. This contract was between Harold, his teacher, and his parents, and if he completed his part of the contract he would be allowed to go to the circus in a neighboring city at the end of the month. Harold was not expected to change his behavior completely, and in fact he had only to earn a happy face (by following the rule for that week for the whole day) for 6 out of a possible 20 days. The expectations for Harold were low at first (that is, a 30 percent behavioral improvement), because he presented an extreme behavioral problem in school. Asking him to be perfect every day (that is, a 100 percent improvement) would have been unrealistic and would have made it impossible for him to succeed and win his reward.

In this type of contract, it is generally best to work on only one

101

Figure 31 RULES CONTRACT

This contract is made between _Harold S._ and _Mr. & Mrs. S._
and _Ms. T._ It states that _Harold_ will learn one new
rule each week, for a period of four weeks. Every day that he doesn't break a rule, he will color
in a happy face for that day. If he earns _6_ happy faces during the four week period,
then he can _go to the circus_.

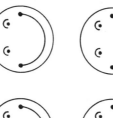
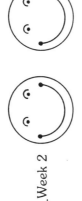

Rule 1: _I will complete all math papers._ Week 1

Rule 2: _I will not fight at recess._ Week 2

Rule 3: _I will get in line when told._ Week 3

Rule 4: _I will do all my homework._ Week 4

Signed: _____

Date: _____

behavior at a time rather than on several at once, and you may wish to work on only one rule for the whole month.

When writing a behavioral contract, make sure to include the following steps:

1. Put down all the people who are involved in the contract.
2. Specify just what each one is supposed to do. Sometimes the adult, as well as the child, will agree to try to change some behavior. Sometimes more than one child will be involved, as when brothers and/or sisters contract not to fight.
3. Write the rules in terms of behaviors that are specific and can be clearly observed. *Do not* write rules which require you to make inferences about the child's behavior, for this will lead to confusion and arguments. For example, don't write, "Bobby will stop fighting"; *instead write,* "Bobby will not fight with his sister at mealtimes."
4. Focus the rules on your priority behaviors and values (see THE PERFECT CHILD GAME). It is better to change one behavior that is really important to you then to change five things that the child does which are less consequential.
5. Make at least two copies of the contract, one for the child and one for the adult who will be monitoring the contract.
6. Before the contract begins, you must decide how you are going to judge whether or not the child has obeyed the rule that day, and this can be done by any of the following methods:

★ **Honor System:** The child decides for himself whether he broke any rules that day or not.

★ **The Buddy System:** Two children who are friends can monitor each other's behavior. Having several children on contracts to change their behaviors will help the child you are working with feel that he is not so different from others. Having children with milder problems or even with no problems on RULES CONTRACTS will also provide your child with role models for successfully changing his behaviors.

★ **Adult Monitoring:** This is the least preferred method, because it sets the adult up as a "watchdog" and a natural antagonist. In many instances, however, this cannot be avoided. If you are the person who must monitor the child's behavior, then remember that you are obligated to be as objective as possible. You are not helping the child if you ignore him when he breaks rules any more than if you are too strict. Help the child understand that you are on his side, and give him hints on how he can change his behavior. The following activities in this section should give you some good ideas on what specific skills your child needs to fultill his contract.

103

sorting out rules

Begin this series of activities with a frank discussion of rules with the child. Too many times adults forget to take the child's opinions and viewpoints into account, only to find out later that the child has a much better understanding of his problems than they gave him credit for. Talk about the importance of rules as they relate to the child and the problems that occur when rules are broken or ignored.

The purpose of this game is to identify the rules that are most important to the child and the adults around him and to be able to assign priorities to them. Write down on a sheet of paper ten rules that the child knows he should follow. Then discuss which of these rules are really important and which are more trivial. Number the rules from 1 to 10, giving the most important rules the lowest numbers and the least important rules the highest numbers. If you have undertaken a RULES CONTRACT with the child, then the rules you have listed in the contract as having the highest priority will have the lowest numbers.

HOW TO MAKE THE GAME

To play this game, you will need to make ten Rule Cards. Follow the instructions carefully, since these cards will be used for all the activities described in this chapter.

1. Take ten 5 × 8 cards and draw a line down the center of each one to divide it in half.
2. On each card, write out in clear simple language one rule from the list you just compiled.
3. Turn the card over and draw a line down the center of the back too.
4. In pencil write the priority number of each rule, from the list you made, on the back right half of each card.
5. Because some of the children whom you may be working with do not read very well, it is important to give them other ways to remember the rules. This can be done by using simple stick figures and line drawings to illustrate the principle involved in each rule. (see Fig. 32 for an example). Usually you will need to do the drawing, but if possible you should do it with the help of the child so that the figures you draw will be meaningful to him.
6. Another approach is to take an instant picture of the child as he pretends to break the rule and mount the picture on the 5 × 8 card. You will probably need to use some props to make it clear in the picture which rule you are demonstrating.

PLAYING THE GAME

Now give the cards to the child and say, "Put them in order, from the most important to the least important. Put the one that you said was

Figure 32

most important on your left and then put the cards down in order so that the least important one is on your right." When the child has done this, turn the cards over and see if he has remembered the order of importance for the rules. If he has a good memory, the numbers should read correctly from 1 to 10 as he reads from left to right.

Not all children will be able to put all the cards in the right order, even after practice, and your expectations must vary from child to child, depending on their ages and how good their memories are. Below are three variations of sorting games to help the child learn the skill of remembering the relative importance of rules. The easiest game is listed first.

Keep the purpose of the game in mind as you play: The child must remember a set of rules that are important to the adults around him. He should realize that some aspects of his behavior are more important to control than others.

SORTING GAMES

1. **THE ONE RULE TO REMEMBER GAME:** Shuffle the ten cards and have the child pick out the highest-priority rule (numbered 1) which he should be working on. He need only turn the card over to see if he is right. Repeat this game until the child identifies the correct card 100 percent of the time.

2. **THE BIG THREE RULES:** Take two coffee cans, paint them, and label one "Big Three" and the other "Little Seven." Shuffle the cards, and have the child put cards 1 to 3 in the Big Three can and the other cards in the Little Seven can, looking only at the fronts of the cards. Have the child

105

practice finding the three most important rules by himself until he can do it without any difficulty. This sorting game can be varied by using any number of cards and cans.

3. **RULES THAT MAKE YOU FLIP:** This is a way to remember the order of all ten cards. Mark out a circle of ten squares on the floor with chalk, giving each square a number between 1 and 10. Place an X on the floor in the center of the circle of squares. To win the game, the child must flip the right card into the right box. The child gets a point when he can land the right card so that it is at least touching the right square. Of course, he can only look at the front of the card before he flips it, and then he can check his responses by looking at the back. The child wins when he can get five of the ten cards in the correct boxes.

the big rule caper

When the child has completed the preceding games, he should be very familiar with the ten rules that are most important to him. Now it is time to make the rules more meaningful by identifying the consequences of breaking them. Here's how to play THE BIG RULE CAPER.

1. Beginning with Rule 1, discuss with the child what happens when each rule is broken and illustrate the consequence of breaking the rules on the right half of each card (see Fig. 33).

2. Write down, in clear language, a simple sentence or phrase which describes each consequence. Sometimes the consequences of breaking all the rules will be the same, but *usually* there will be different consequences for the high-priority rules than for the low-priority rules. You may want to review the principles of disciplining the child with poor self-control discussed in Chapter 2.

3. Now give the child three new 5 × 8 cards and a clipboard. Explain to the child: "Now we are going to find out about what other people think of your rules, and what happened to them when they broke rules at your age. You will play the part of a detective, looking for the "big rule" that is the one rule that no one should break. We're going to begin by asking three people two questions: "What was the most important rule to you when you were my age?" and "What happened when you broke that rule?" You can ask them other questions too if you like, but stick to the facts. Then give them blank cards and ask them to write the rule most important to them and what happened when they broke the rule, just as you did on your cards. We'll show them one of your cards and ask them

Figure 33

to draw a picture of the rule and the consequence of breaking the rule just as we did.''

For younger children, you can emphasize the game nature of this activity by having them wear a detective badge, interview the suspect, and so forth. With an older child, who might find this babyish, let him play the role of an investigative reporter and don't emphasize props. You'll probably want to begin by having the child interview you and helping him polish up his social skills. Keep the interviews short, about 5 to 10 minutes, and naturally, give the person to be interviewed an idea of the purpose of the activity beforehand. It is a good idea to have the child begin by interviewing adults and older children, but if he is socially sophisticated, he may want to interview classmates and other friends as well.

When all three interviews are completed, the child should compare his cards with the new cards he has collected. Let him see if by comparing them, he can find the "big rule" that is most important to people. Emphasize to the child that: ***Everyone breaks rules at some time in his or her life. Everyone has to live with the consequences of breaking rules. People agree that some rules are more important than others to obey.***

what others think of your rules

In the last two games, you laid groundwork for helping the child to identify what rules are important to him and to others and why they are important. Now it is time to have the child try to understand just *where* and *when* these rules apply. The next game explains how to construct and play card games that will help the child remember the rules that should be of most concern to him. Try to make these games fun, for that will be one of the prime motivations in getting your child to practice the skills he now lacks in learning to obey rules.

Making the Game

1. Cut the 5 × 8 cards that you made in the last two games in half; this will give you 20 playing cards—10 with rules on them and 10 with consequences.
2. Make 10 more playing cards of the same size (five new 5 × 8 cards cut in half).
3. On these 10 new cards show the time and place where the child normally breaks rules (see Fig. 34). We will call these *When and Where* cards. Photographs can be used to show the place where the child most often breaks the rules.

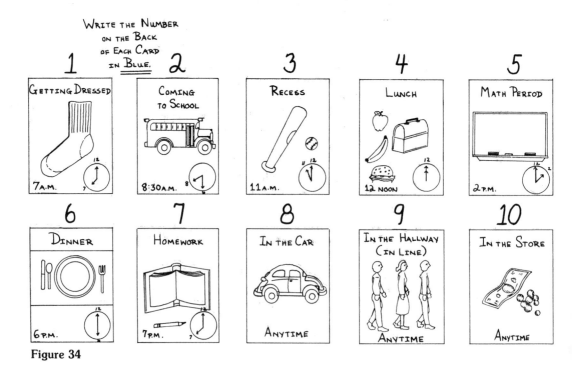

Figure 34

4. The time when the child usually breaks the rule should be written out and indicated by a clock face.

5. When the cards are ready, arrange them in a row in front of the child in order of the time of day, beginning with the cards showing time early in the morning and ending with the cards designating evening times.

6. Put the cards without exact times last (for example cards 8, 9, and 10 in Fig. 34).

7. Now using blue pencil put the numbers 1 to 10 on the backs of these cards to designate their sequence.

You now have a deck of 30 cards, 10 with rules, 10 with consequences, and 10 with times and places that the child you are working with most often breaks rules.

HOW TO PLAY THE GAME

The child must now try to understand when and where he must play by the rules that he has identified. Direct the child to take the ten rule cards and place them directly below the Where and When cards that you just made, which he thinks show where and when he is most likely to break each rule (see Fig. 35). Discuss with the child the placement of each card. You will probably find that the child sees himself as breaking several rules at the same time and place, and that the ten rule cards will tend to cluster around three or four Where and When cards. This is a positive sign and should make helping the child an easier task, for it will allow you to target certain time periods and places in which the child needs help in learning self-control.

Now say to the child, "The object of this game is simple. You want each grown-up to place the cards in the same order as they appear now, with all the numbers matching in each column. Of course the grown-ups will only be able to look at the face of each card.

"Remember that we put a blue number on the back of each When and Where card. [Turn these cards over to show the child.] Now we will put this same number in red pencil on the back of each rule card and in green pencil on the consequence card that goes with it. [see Fig. 35]. Then we'll ask your mother, your father, and your teacher [or any three significant adults] to play the same game and to put the right rule and consequence cards under the same Where and When cards as you did. For every time they place the same rule and consequence cards under the same Where and When, you win a point. Since there are three people, each trying to match twenty cards, a perfect score would be 60 points, but if you can just get 20 points you will get a special prize. Now look at the way you placed the cards one more time and see if there are any changes that you want to make before we begin."

Then go to each adult and line up the Where and When cards in

109

Figure 35

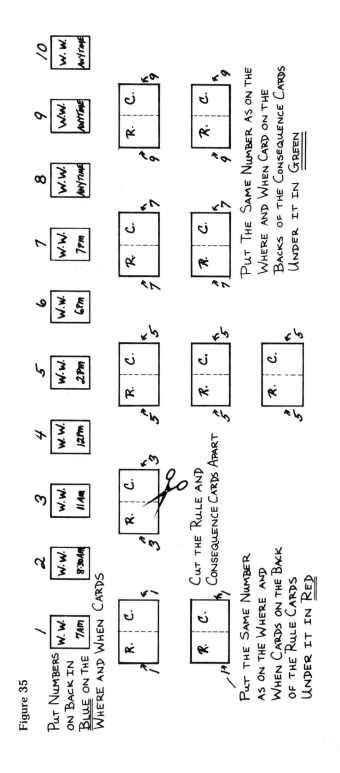

PUT NUMBERS ON BACK IN BLUE ON THE WHERE AND WHEN CARDS

1 W.W. 7AM
2 W.W. 8:30AM
3 W.W. 11AM
4 W.W. 12PM
5 W.W. 2PM
6 W.W. 6PM
7 W.W. 7PM
8 W.W. ANYTIME
9 W.W. ANYTIME
10 W.W. ANYTIME

PUT THE SAME NUMBER AS ON THE WHERE AND WHEN CARDS ON THE BACK OF THE RULE CARDS UNDER IT IN RED

CUT THE RULE AND CONSEQUENCE CARDS APART

PUT THE SAME NUMBER AS ON THE WHERE AND WHEN CARD ON THE BACKS OF THE CONSEQUENCE CARDS UNDER IT IN GREEN

order by the numbers on the back of each card. You say to the adult:
"The top row of cards shows times and places at which Bobby [or
whatever the child's name is] thinks he breaks rules. Here are 20 more
cards; ten show the rules that are broken most often, and ten show the
consequences of breaking these rules. Put each rule card below the
When and Where card that you think corresponds to the time and place
at which Bobby is most likely to break each rule. Then put each Consequence card next to the rule card you think it belongs to. Remember that
the Consequence card shows what happens to him when he breaks the
rule."

Now turn all the cards over. Going down each column, give the
adult one point for each card that matches the top card in that column.
The numbers of the cards marked in green and red should match those of
the cards marked in blue. Score each adult's responses on the score sheet
provided for you in Fig. 36. The higher the score, the more agreement
there is between the child's perceptions of his rule system and the
perceptions of the adults around him. Total the points for each When and
Where card across the rows and then calculate a grand total. A grand total
of 20 points is good—a total over 30 is excellent.

Figure 36 RESPONSE SHEET FOR "WHAT OTHERS THINK OF YOUR RULES"

INSTRUCTIONS: Give each adult 1 pt. for each card he/she places under the correct When & Where card (for example it will have the same number on the back as the When & Where card it is under).

	Adult #1	Adult #2	Adult #3		Total Correct
Where & When Card 1					
2					
3					
4					
5					
6					
7					
8					
9					
10					
	Total for Adult #1	Total for Adult #2	Total for Adult #3		Grand Total

Hobbies: the road to good work habits

Anna Freud has noted that hobbies are developmentally halfway between play and work, sharing certain characteristics of both. Like play, they are pleasurable, comparatively free from external pressures, and removed (but not too far) from the child's basic drives. Like work, hobbies require important cognitive and emotional skills, including planning, delay of gratification, and ability to tolerate frustration.

The acquisition of a hobby for the child without self-control is a way to break into the behavior cycle of failure, frustration, and underachievement. Hobbies give the child with poor self-control an opportunity to develop skill areas that directly translate into good study habits, yet the child is removed from the competitive pressures of school. Perhaps for the first time, the child can learn to take pride in the things he can do and produce at his hobby, and he can develop a positive identity with other people who share the same interests.

Three major types of hobbies are presented in this section: collecting, craft hobbies, and performing hobbies. When deciding which type of hobby a child should pursue, you should consider that the hobbies presented here are in a sequential order according to the level of difficulty of cognitive and emotional skills required. However, you must also take into account the interests of the child, for he may perform at his worst in things that he considers to be boring, and yet he may show achievements that you never thought possible if he selects a hobby that he really loves.

113

choosing what to collect

Collecting is considered the easiest hobby for children, because it is based on feelings that are almost instinctual. Nearly every child collects something at some time. Like many other primates, humans have a hoarding instinct, which makes them want to acquire and possess material objects whether they have a clear value or not. Although it is sometimes hard to understand why some people collect what they do, the repetition involved in the collecting process—and the sense of accomplishment involved when the collection is assembled—cannot be underestimated as a motivating factor in helping children. To begin with, a collecting hobby must be selected that is practical, affordable, and attractive to the child you are working with. Make a list of collections that meet these criteria, and have the child select the one which is most interesting to him. This list might include:

autographs	dolls	miniature items of all kinds
bottles	flags	patches
bubble gum cards	insects	pressed flowers
buttons	leaves	rocks
cans	marbles	shells
		special photographs

The Collection Selection Chart shown in Fig. 37 may be helpful in determining the best type of collection for the child. Write the five hobbies the child finds most attractive in the left-hand column and rate each one as to its positive features. The hobby with the most points is the best one to start with.

the collecting process

Even though all children like to collect things, you can still anticipate that the impulsive child will have trouble with his hobby. Collecting takes patience, a sense of organization, and an ability to stick with a project. These are qualities that impulsive children lack. For this reason, the adult must work closely with the child, guiding him through each step of the collection process. Set aside a place and a time for the hobby and work on it regularly. Plan what you are going to do at each session, and make sure the child gains a sense of accomplishment by completing each task in

Figure 37   THE COLLECTION SELECTION CHART

Collections I might like (Examples)	Inexpensive	Someone I like has this hobby	Sounds like fun	I have thought of this before	I would be proud of my hobby	Total
Coins						
Leaves						
Buttons						
Stamps						
Pins						
Stones						
Toy Soldiers						

The collection with the most checks should be the one the child will most likely enjoy and stick to.

the time you have allowed. Here are six activities which are a part of most collecting hobbies. Next to each activity is an estimate of how long the activity will take. Keep a record of how much time the child spends at each activity. How does it compare with the time he spends at schoolwork? If you can make the schoolwork as interesting and active as the collecting process, you will see an increase in the child's attention span in the classroom.

1. Do research on the hobby.
Activity: Go to the library and check out two books on the hobby.   30 minutes
Activity: Send away for free literature on the hobby. Have the   10 minutes
child dictate two or more letters to you, addressed to national clubs, catalog publishers, government agencies related to the hobby, or other sources of information.
Activity: Visit displays of similar collections at museums, stores,   30 minutes
fairs, or elsewhere.

2. Decide on the best way to gather the collection.
Activity: Take a nature walk, Make sure you go to a place that is   30 minutes
very likely to have what you are looking for; otherwise you will frustrate the child.
Activity: Go shopping. If the hobby the child has selected costs   30 minutes
money, make sure he has the opportunity to earn an allowance by doing simple chores. When you go shopping for the hobby, do not combine the outing with other shopping, for this will bore the child and make the experience less positive. Instead, plan to take the time when you can fully concentrate on helping the child do his collecting.

Activity: Arrange swap sessions. If the child has friends who have   60 minutes
the same hobby, you might be able to arrange a time for them to
trade various items from their collections. It is generally best to
have an adult organize and supervise these sessions to avoid
squabbles and bad feelings.

organizing the collection

Once the collection is under way, consideration must begin about
how the collectibles are to be organized and displayed. For most collec-
tors, this process is even more enjoyable than the actual acquisition of the
collection, for it involves a higher level of cognitive processes and of
appreciation. For these same reasons, the organization and display of the
collection is important for the impulsive child.

The organization and display of the collection is an ongoing process
that begins when the first few items are acquired. The child should begin
by choosing how the collection can best be displayed. Here are a few
ideas:

* **Scrapbook:** This can be made fairly inexpensively and can have
highly aesthetic results. The scrapbook can be subdivided into categories
within the collection (for example, types of leaves, types of autographs,
types of pictures), with one page used for each classification. Before the
collection is inserted into the scrapbook, all the items should first be
sorted into envelopes or boxes which identify each of the categories.
When the child has enough items to fill a page of the scrapbook, he
should lay out the items on the page and arrange them in a way that best
shows off the collection. You can help make the scrapbook even more
aesthetic by lettering the pages or the cover, using a stencil or press-on
letters which are available at local stationery stores.

* **Box display:** Three-dimensional small items (such as buttons,
small dolls, or rocks) can best be displayed in one or more boxes that are
subdivided. Decorated egg cartons make good display boxes, as do
many candy boxes and cigar boxes which come with sectional dividers.
Most variety stores carry a wide assortment of plastic boxes (for notions,
nuts and bolts, and fishing tackle) which make very attractive display
cases.

* **Frames/collages:** Many small two-dimensional items can be
used as wall decorations by either framing them or mounting them on
poster board to make a collage. Organize the collection into categories
(sizes of butterflies, teams of baseball cards, colors of ribbon) and mount
each category in a separate frame or collage.

★ **Filing box:** Collecting may also lend itself to various filing systems using index cards or small envelopes. Filing is an excellent organizing skill for the impulsive child to master. Coins may be filed by date, buttons may be sewn to index cards and filed by size and shape, and leaves may be filed alphabetically by the names of the trees from which they came.

CRAFT HOBBIES

put the shirt on your back

Crafts are particularly good activities for the impulsive child because they have a clear value. Because they result in functional products (for example, pencil holders, planters, toys) they are more meaningful to impulsive children than free-form art. Because craft products can be used as gifts or sold at fairs, they may actually have a monetary value, which makes the child feel that there is a concrete worth to what he can produce.

Developmentally, craft hobbies are slightly more difficult for the impulsive child than collecting hobbies, for they generally require more patience and concentration. There are many good books now on the market which describe how to make simple and inexpensive craft items; some of my favorites are listed in the Suggested Reading section.

Special considerations should be kept in mind when teaching crafts to the impulsive child, however. Keep things simple. Begin with craft projects that involve just a few materials which are not difficult for the child to work with. Choose crafts that are aesthetically pleasing in their nature rather than dependent on the creativity of the child. All children with a poor self-concept will tend to devalue their work, and will be displeased with something that does not look like a finished job.

Accept the child's viewpoint of his work. Be encouraging, but don't argue with him if he doesn't like it or even if he decides to destroy it. Work with him to get the finished product just the way he wants it.

Tie-dyeing T-shirts is a great beginner craft activity because it is virtually a foolproof project, and it can be completed in one step. Make sure that both you and the child are wearing old clothes and that you have a work space such that you will not be concerned if the child makes a mess. Remember that even professional artists and craftsmen must forget about neatness and order while they create, and you should expect no more from an impulsive child.

To make these colorful shirts, follow these steps:

1. Take a plain white T-shirt and gather up the material into five to ten bunches.
2. Tie each bunch with a piece of string or a rubber band.
3. Dip the entire shirt into a solution of a clothes dye, following the instructions on the package.
4. After the T-shirt is completely dry, remove all the knots and you will have created your own original design.

If the child enjoys this hobby, let him experiment using two or more dyes and dyeing other types of clothes (such as scarves or skirt material). These products make excellent presents. Most craft and hobby stores will have kits and books on other ways to decorate clothing (for example, iron-on pictures, water colors, or studs for blue jeans).

beautiful boxes

In this activity, the child must work on a project that cannot be completed in one session. The child with poor self-control must learn to work without immediate rewards and still must be motivated to complete the project. Making a decoupage box will involve a minimum of three 15-minute sessions and may be stretched to as many as six sessions. As in the previous activity, you should keep a record of how long the child is able to participate in the craft without being distracted. Each session should have a clear beginning and end and should take place at approximately the same time on successive days. Again, you should take the child's increasing attention span as a benchmark of his potential school performance.

To begin this project, present the child with boxes of different sizes and have him select one that could serve a specific function, such as storing pencils, crayons, small toys, gloves, or other items. Have him paint the box with poster paint and let it dry. Then have him paste on magazine pictures that are related to the function of the box, such as pictures of children playing for a box that will hold toys or pictures of people working for a box that will hold school supplies. The child should let the pictures dry and then brush three to six coats of liquid glue over the entire box, letting each layer of glue dry completely before applying the next layer. The more layers of glue that are applied, the more the box will have a glossy, polished look.

118

For the purpose of this discussion, I will distinguish performing *hobbies* from performing *arts* such as music or dance, since the former require no special talents and the latter are characterized by hard work and practice, which would typically be beyond the ability of the impulsive child.*

The performing hobbies in this section, puppetry and magic, were selected because they are extremely popular with children and yet can offer activities at a wide range of skill levels. They were chosen as the last activities in the book because they require the child to have developed many of the skills for self-control mentioned earlier. Specifically, the child will need to acquire the abilities to practice, plan, control his motor movements, and estimate time intervals before he can be successful in a performing hobby. The new skills that will be worked on in this subsection will help the child to gain control in communication, social confidence, and the ability to get attention in a socially appropriate manner.

puppet power

Puppets have been used for some time in helping children to communicate their problems. Children will often have a puppet reveal what is on their minds when they are otherwise silent. While spontaneous puppet play is beneficial for children in allowing them to express their true feelings, that is not the primary goal of the puppet play for the impulsive child, who already acts spontaneously and expresses his feelings too much. In this activity we are more concerned that the child learn a socially appropriate way to get attention. Specifically, the impulsive child must learn how to get people to laugh, not at him or his problem but at puppets that are under his control.

Make a boy and a girl puppet. These may be finger puppets, stick puppets, hand puppets, or paper-doll puppets according to your preference (see Figs. 8 and 38). Construct a stage by draping a dark-colored table cloth or sheet over a small bridge table so that the cloth flows down to the floor on at least one side. The child can sit behind the table, hidden from the audience by the cloth, and perform on top of the table.

*This is not always the case, however, and it is not uncommon to see children with different handicaps who have innate artistic talent. If this is the case with your child, you should have him pursue these talents, following the relationship principles outlined in the introduction.

Figure 38

— USE A STYROFOAM BALL TO MAKE THE HEAD

— USE A HANDKERCHIEF FOR THE BODY

— USE CUT-OUT FIGURES FROM MAGAZINES GLUED TO HEAVY DUTY POSTER PAPER

CUT OUT HOLES FOR TWO FINGERS

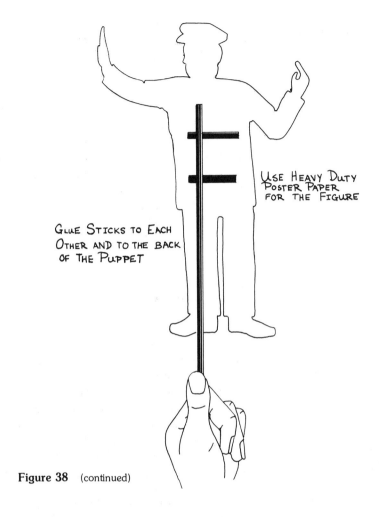

USE HEAVY DUTY
POSTER PAPER
FOR THE FIGURE

GLUE STICKS TO EACH
OTHER AND TO THE BACK
OF THE PUPPET

Figure 38 (continued)

Now you must make a script for the puppet show. You should tape-record it so that the child can concentrate on the movement of the puppets rather than on memorizing dialogue. Here are some ideas of ways to make scripts, ranked by order of difficulty.

★ **Talk songs:** Many popular songs tell a funny story and can be the script for the entire play.

★ **Joke and riddle books:** One puppet can tell jokes and riddles to the others which are taken directly from popular joke books. You can add sound effects to the tape, which will also get laughs.

★ **Record a personal story:** Perhaps the child knows a funny story, or has a friend or relative who is a good story teller. Record the story as it is

121

told, asking the speaker to talk slowly (keep the story to about five minutes). Music may be added at the beginning and end of the story for a "professional" effect.

Summary of Steps

1. Select a "play" to tape-record.
2. Make the appropriate puppets you will need.
3. Have the child practice the show in front of a mirror, suggesting ways to move the puppets along with the script.
4. When the child is sure of himself, make invitations for a few (not more than four) people to the show.
5. The child may wish to pursue his hobby by making other kinds of puppets, making more elaborate sets and stages, and inviting friends to take some of the roles.

making magic

Magic is very popular with children and the learning and performing of magic tricks coincidentally involves many cognitive and social skills that are of great benefit to the impulsive child. When a child feels that he has mastered a trick, he feels that he knows something that no one else does, and this adds a new dimension to his self-concept. In learning the trick, the impulsive child must coordinate his thoughts with his actions and must develop a sense of time and timing, which these children typically lack. The child's natural motivation to master and show off the trick will make him practice and practice—a new way to learn for the impulsive child, who typically gets bored easily. When performing a magic trick, the impulsive child, who usually is seen as in the way, suddenly becomes a leader of a group and learns to get attention in a very appropriate way.

There are hundreds of simple tricks that a child can easily master and use to astound his friends. I have selected one which can be learned by a second grader in just a few minutes, and yet is fun to do and fun to watch. In choosing the first trick for an impulsive child to learn, I suggest that you go to a local toy store and purchase one that is commercially available. There are also many books on magic available at your local library which show children how to make many of their own tricks. However, most of these books are aimed at the older child and trying to learn the tricks may be frustrating for the impulsive child. In any event, the adult should follow these steps in teaching magic to an impulsive child:

1. Learn the trick yourself first. Make sure that the trick is easy enough for the child to learn before you give it to him. Otherwise, he will become frustrated and disappointed.

2. Help the child with his practice. Be a good and instructive audience. Show him how to practice in front of the mirror and help him to analyze the best way to present the trick.

3. Keep the child from showing his trick to others before he is ready. The impulsive child will quite naturally want to show others his trick as soon as he has any of the rudiments mastered; however, it is important to make sure he has practiced it thoroughly first. Teach him about the importance of choosing the right time and place to show a trick, so that he can keep his secrets safely.

THE DANGEROUS EGG TRICK

You will need: an apron
3 raw eggs
1 hard-boiled egg
1 colorful handkerchief
1 kitchen strainer
a flat tray

1. Tell the audience that some magicians can read minds but you can read eggs.

2. Say, "All these eggs look alike, but three of them are raw and one of them is hard-boiled. When these eggs are spinning, the hard-boiled egg will tell me where it is."

3. Select a volunteer from the audience to assist you. Tell the volunteer to spin each egg with equal force alone on the tray.

4. Watch the eggs very closely. *The hard-boiled egg will spin much faster and much longer.* This is because the liquid inside the raw eggs causes friction inside the shell and slows the egg down.

5. Pick up the kitchen strainer, hold it over the handkerchief, and say, "Now I will ask my assistant to break the egg that I point to over my mother's best handkerchief. If I have selected the hard-boiled one, it will stay in the strainer. If I am wrong, my mother is going to be very mad."

123

Practice this trick several times in the kitchen, until you can pick out the hard-boiled egg every time. Just in case you do make a mistake, perform the trick in an area that can be cleaned up easily. And don't worry if you goof. Every magician makes a mistake sometimes. If you have chosen a raw egg by mistake say, "Well, I told you that eggs talk to me. But I didn't say that they tell the truth." Then clean up the egg as quickly as possible and go on to another trick. The audience will think that you are very funny.

Suggested readings

The list of suggested readings is divided into two sections: **Theory** has been compiled for those who wish to explore the theoretical concepts behind this book; **Activity** is for those who wish to pursue more activities designed to help the impulsive child.

THEORY

ARNOLD, EUGENE *Helping Parents Help Their Children.* New York: Brunner/Mazel, 1978.

> I have found this a particularly helpful book because it focuses on the parent's point of view. There is a section on the major approaches to working through parents, another on helping parents cope with specific problems of children (including hyperactive and aggressive children), and another which focuses on helping parents who themselves have problems (for example, divorced parents, teenage mothers, and adoptive parents.)

BENSON, HERBERT *The Relaxation Response.* New York: Avon Books, 1975.

> In this popular book, Benson gives a convincing argument for the benefits of transcendental meditation. The technique is described simply and concisely.

125

SUGGESTED READINGS

DODSON, FITZHUGH *How to Discipline with Love.* A Signet Book. New York: NAL, 1978.

This manual for parents is a good summary of the humanistic approach to disciplining children. The author recognizes that not all techniques work with all children and offers a sufficient variety of discipline strategies that most parents will find at least one section to help them relate to their child on more positive terms.

FINE, MARVIN, ed. *Principles and Techniques of Intervention with Hyperactive Children.* Springfield, Ill.: Charles C. Thomas, 1977.

This is the best summary of research on hyperactive children that I have found. The introductory chapter by Fine and the chapter on educational management by Norma J. Dyck are especially helpful in getting an overview of the problem.

FREUD, ANNA *The Writings of Anna Freud,* (volume VI) *Normality and Pathology in Childhood: Assessments of Development.* New York: International Universities Press, Inc., 1965.

Although this book does not specifically address children who have problems in self-control, it nevertheless gives such a classic analytic developmental framework for understanding children that it is important reading for the clinician who wants to get a perspective on childhood problems.

MARTIN, GARY, and JOSEPH PEAR *Behavior Modification: What It Is and How to Do It.* Englewood Cliffs, N.J.: Prentice-Hall, 1978.

This is a good, clearly written review of the most common behavior modification techniques used today.

MEICHENBAUM, DONALD *Cognitive Behavior Modification.* New York: Plenum, 1977.

This book reviews the major research in the use of cognitive strategies to modify behavior. The review offers dozens of creative treatment strategies for children and adults with a variety of problems.

ROTH, JUNE *Cooking for Your Hyperactive Child.* Chicago: Contemporary Books, Inc., 1977.

This book provides a wide variety of recipes for additive-free cooking, including a sensitivity checklist for each recipe so that the reader can easily plan a menu that rotates the basic food groups. Some allergists claim that this procedure prevents new food sensitivities from forming.

126

SLOANE, HOWARD N. *The Good Kid Book.* New York: NAL, 1979.

A slick, original behavior modification manual for parents who have children with discipline problems. The chapters are organized around common, everyday problems, which makes it easy to find a program to match with your child's problems. Some of the programs may be a little technical for parents, but the author gives such sound and clear advice that even the psychological novice should be able to benefit from this approach.

ACTIVITY BOOKS

BERESFORD, MARGARET *How to Make Puppets and Teach Puppetry,* London: Mills and Boon Ltd., 1966.

This is one of the better books on puppetry that I have found. It explains how to make several different kinds of puppets and includes a section on how puppets can be linked to other areas of the school curriculum. Eight plays "written and acted by children" are also included.

FIAROTTA, PHYLLIS, and NOEL FIAROTTA *Be What You Want to Be!* New York: Workman Publishing Co., 1977.

The Fiarottas have published several craft activity books for children, all of which are original and well illustrated. This is my favorite because of its theme: making props and costumes to play-act different types of careers.

GILLIS, RUTH, JR. *Children's Books for Times of Stress, an Annotated Bibliography.* Bloomington/London: Indiana University Press, 1978.

Many professionals advocate that children with problems can learn about themselves from reading about other children and families with difficulties similar to their own. If you think a child can benefit from this approach, called *bibliotherapy,* then you should begin with this or a similar bibliography.

HODGSON, HARRIET W. *"I Made it Myself!"* New York: Warner B. Lansky Books, Inc., 1979.

Of the many books now available for children on how to make their own toys and crafts, this is one of the best for impulsive, active children. I like it because the toys are simple and require a minimum of manual dexterity. The illustrations are excellent and easy to follow.

127

MADARAS, LYNDA *Child's Play.* Culver City, Calif.: Peace Press, Inc., 1977.

This is a wide-ranging activity book for children and contains good illustrations and photographs. I particularly like it for the sections on how to start a play group and how to build a playground from junk.

ORLICK, TERRY *The Cooperative Sports and Games Book.* New York: Pantheon, 1978.

This book suggests activities well suited to the most pressing needs of the very active child—games which teach physical and social controls. There are some terrific ideas in this book.

PALMER, BRUCE *Making Children's Furniture and Play Structures.* New York: Workman Publishing Co., 1974.

Palmer tells how to make stools, tables, chairs, desks, beds, storage units, and other structures from corrugated cardboard. There are many projects to keep the impulsive, active child interested and working.

SHEPHERD, WALTER *The Big Book of Mazes and Labyrinths.* New York: Dover, 1973.

This is one of dozens of maze books on the market. I particularly like it because of its original art work. The mazes are fairly difficult, however, and would not be appropriate for children under ten or eleven, or children with visual-motor problems. Simpler maze books are available in most book stores and have themes such as superheroes, space ships, and monsters.

SIMON, SIDNEY B., LELAND W. HOWE, and HOWARD KIRSCHENBAUM *Values Clarification: A Handbook of Practical Strategies for Teachers and Students.* New York: Hart Publishing Co., Inc., 1972.

This widely read book has 70 strategies to help you think about what you believe, what you think, and how you behave. Many of the strategies can be adapted to help children with problems, as well as their parents and teachers.

STEED, FREIDA REED *A Special Picture Cookbook.* Lawrence, Kans.: H & H Enterprises, Inc., 1977.

This is a simple, well-illustrated, step-by-step guide to teaching children how to prepare basic food items. Each recipe begins with an illustration showing the ingredients that are needed and the cooking steps (mixing, cutting, and so forth) that are involved in the recipe.

STEIN, SARA BONNETT *The Kid's Kitchen Takeover.* New York: Workman Publishing Co., 1975.

This is one of my favorite cookbooks for children because it goes far beyond food preparation and makes the kitchen into a living laboratory. There are all kinds of interesting activities and experiments, most of which require some adult guidance for the child with poor self-control.

THE AMAZING LIFE GAMES COMPANY *Good Cents: Every Kid's Guide to Making Money.* Boston: Houghton Mifflin Co., 1974.

This is one of my favorite activity books for children. It is funny, creative, and gives some terrific ideas to help them make and handle money.

ZUBROWSKI, BERNIE *Milk Carton Blocks.* Boston/Toronto: Little, Brown, 1979.

This is one of a series of books called Children's Museum Activity Books. Construction is a positive activity for the impulsive child who is more frequently known for destructive activities. This book makes building into a creative learning activity which should be fun for both children and adults.

Appendixes

BEHAVIORAL OBJECTIVES FOR TEACHERS

To incorporate the games in this book into an effective curriculum, you will need to match the games to specific behavioral objectives for each child. If a child has been identified by the school system as handicapped, then the behavioral objectives will be part of that child's individual educational plan (IEP) and will normally be approved by an interdisciplinary team of appropriate professionals and the child's parents or guardians.

The following are suggested behavioral objectives for each game, listed in the same developmental order as they appear in the book. If you already have a specific objective in mind for a child you are working with (or his parents), then you should read over the objectives listed below and determine which one most clearly matches your intentions. Then find the game by using the index and read the introduction to the chapter in which the game is described. This will give you the context of the purpose of the game and should help you evaluate your selection. You should feel free to modify any games to meet the child's needs.

TARGETS   Adults working to help the child will be able to assign priorities to his problem behaviors and pinpoint the one behavior that is most significant to his development.

CLUES AND CUES   The adults working with the child will be able to determine cues (antecedents) which predict the child's behaviors.

RELAXING ABOUT THINGS   The adults working with the child will be able to approach the child calmly when administering discipline.

MIRROR, MIRROR ON THE WALL   The adults working with the child will learn to reflect for the child his own feelings and behaviors when he misbehaves.

LET THE PUNISHMENT OVERFIT THE CRIME	The adults working with the child will learn to select appropriate punishments for the child with problems in self-control.
PICTURE, PERFECT POSITIVE BEHAVIOR	The adults working with the child will learn to reinforce positive behaviors.
THE MAGIC SEAT	The child will be able to remain seated in a chair for 15 to 30 minutes during highly stimulating activities.
THE BEST SEAT IN THE HOUSE	The child will increase the number of times that he independently chooses to be in a seat.
A STICKY CHAIR	The child will go to his seat more readily when asked.
THE ACTIVITY MENU	The child will increase his attention span at work-type activities.
FINGER-PUPPET DANCES	The child will increase his finger coordination.
ART POWER	The child will improve his hand and eye coordination.
THE GAME OF ADAPTATION	The child will improve specific fine motor tasks, such as writing and cutting, using adaptive equipment.
BASIC CONCEPTS BASEBALL	The child will learn eleven basic spatial concepts.
SOMEONE SAYS	The child will more readily follow specific oral directions.
SAY IT WITH SIGNS	The child will learn to follow an adult's directions through gestures.
THE SECRET TREASURE MAP GAME	The child will learn to use a map to follow sequential directions.
FINDING THE WAY TO WORK	The child will learn to use a map to be in the right place at the right time.
THE SECRET SPY GAME	The child will learn to use a map as a reminder to do chores around the house.
COOKING UP NEW SKILLS	The child will learn to follow sequential written directions.
SLOW THINGS	The child will learn to slow down his movements in organized activities.
GUESSING TIME	The child will learn to estimate time intervals when doing work.
LET THE CLOCK BEAT YOU	The child will be able to increase his concentration over longer time intervals.

131

TIME ON YOUR HANDS	The child will learn to use a watch to be on time for important events of the day.
THE PROBLEM, THE PEG, AND THE CLOCK	The child will be able to assess his strengths and weaknesses as related to his impulsivity.
AMAZE ME	The child will be able to perform unrelated intermediate steps while solving a maze.
AMAZE ME AGAIN	The child will use a cue card to identify and correct the impulsive mistakes he makes while solving a maze.
THE ONE MORE TIME MAZE	The child will be able to solve a (maze) problem in less time and with fewer errors by thinking out loud.
AMAZING HOMEWORK	The child will demonstrate a more reflective approach to problem solving in his independent work.
THINKING NUMBERS OUT LOUD	The child will be able to identify his mistakes in math problems caused by his impulsivity.
THE PERFECT CHILD GAME	The adults working with the child learn their priority rules for the child.
THE RULES CONTRACT	The child will break specific rules less frequently.
SORTING OUT RULES	The child will be able to identify the rules that are most important to him.
THE BIG RULE CAPER	The child will be able to identify the rules that are most important to the people around him.
WHAT OTHERS THINK OF YOUR RULES	The child will be able to identify where and when he breaks rules.
CHOOSING WHAT TO COLLECT	The child will choose a collecting hobby.
THE COLLECTING PROCESS	The child will pursue a series of activities related to his hobby with a minimum degree of supervision.
ORGANIZING THE COLLECTION	The child will demonstrate specific organizing skills in displaying his collection.
PUT THE SHIRT ON YOUR BACK	The child will be able to produce a craft item, working 15 minutes without being distracted.

132

BEAUTIFUL BOXES	The child will be able to make a craft item by working on it for three separate ten-minute sessions.
PUPPET POWER	The child will be able to perform a ten-minute puppet show and make the audience laugh.
MAKING MAGIC	The child will be able to learn, practice, and perform a magic trick.

APPENDIX B

ANSWERS TO THE LET THE PUNISHMENT OVERFIT THE CRIME GAME

1. Restitutional correction   b
   Positive practice   i
2. Restitutional correction   c
   Positive practice   g
3. Restitutional correction   a
   Positive practice   e
4. Restitutional correction   f
   Positive practice   j
5. Restitutional correction   d
   Positive practice   h

Index

137